Born in Alnwick, Northumberland in 1977, Joanne Goodwin-Worton has lived in Staffordshire most of her life surrounded by her family and friends. Jo is an extremely proud mother to two grown-up sons, Lewis and Oliver.

Jo married her late-husband in 2008 but it was in 2018 that her life changed irreversibly when he was diagnosed with Upper Gastro-Oesophageal Cancer. What followed was an extraordinary and brave leap of faith into a new way of living, including a new career, going back to university to complete a degree and ultimately finding love again.

Jo's journey showcases her tenacity and stoicism for life and her commitment to living life to the fullest and ultimately using her experience to help people who become a carer of a loved one with cancer and/or experience bereavement.

Jo was married to her best friend for twelve years before he was given the diagnosis of stage four Gastro-Oesophageal Cancer in 2018. He passed away in 2019 after a life-changing journey including his diagnosis, treatment and prognosis.

This is Jo's uncensored real-life journey as a carer through the cancer pathway and how she coped with the emotions and expectations from his diagnosis to her bereavement and grief.

There are so many people I would like to thank for helping me become me again but in particular my friends and family who have truly been remarkable in my journey.

Lewis & Oliver – You have always and will always be my greatest achievement. I am so very proud of you both; I have so much pride and love for your stoicism and bravery. Dream big and always seize the day, knowing that Jay would be immensely proud of you both and will always be guiding you.

Gareth – You hold my heart, acknowledge my scar and love me even more than I thought possible. I feel so blessed to have met someone who loves me for just being me. You have always believed in me and never questioned my crazy ideas. I truly cannot wait to see where our lives take us. I love you.

Mum & Dad – You are and will always be my heroes, you taught me the importance of hard work and always following my dreams. You have been through so much but you have always been there for me. I just hope you know how grateful I am to have your love and support and for being such amazing role-models.

To all my amazing life-long friends – When I broke and when I fell, you picked me up and you held me until I could stand again on my own two feet. Even now when I have a 'wobble' you are there for me. You are truly exceptional and I feel blessed to have you in my life. Special thanks to:

Sarah
Nikkie'Momoa'
Sharon'Momoa'
The 'Golden Oldies' – Darren, Dave, Phil, Pete and Neil
Paul & Emma

Above all though, there is one person I do need to thank and that is Jay. You were loved by many but liked by all who met you. It was my honour to have been your best friend and wife. You brought the boys up as your own and shaped them into the young adults they are today and I know without a doubt that your influence has guided them to a bright future. You left us far too early and we will never understand why cancer had to choose you. It's very unfair and very cruel that your life was cut short before you had even begun to really live. No one can bring you back but what we can do is honour your life by living ours and to make living worthwhile and precious.

You were always and will always be the most wonderful person, this world is a sadder place for losing you but a happier place for knowing that you made a difference to so many people and changed their lives for the better, forever.

James 'Jay' Goodwin
21.12.1977 – 25.07.2019

Joanne Goodwin-Worton

CARING FOR CANCER, THE REAL JOURNEY

AUSTIN MACAULEY PUBLISHERS™

LONDON • CAMBRIDGE • NEW YORK • SHARJAH

A CIP catalogue record for this title is available from the British Library.

ISBN 9781787108271 (Paperback)
ISBN 9781398442962 (ePub e-book)

www.austinmacauley.com

First Published 2022
Austin Macauley Publishers Ltd®
1 Canada Square
Canary Wharf
London
E14 5AA

Thank you to all the dedicated teams who cared for Jay:

The amazing Upper GI team at the NHS University Hospital of North Midlands Hospital, in particular:

Consultant Oesophagogastric Surgeon – Mr Jagadesham
Clinical Nurse Specialists – Sarah & Tina
UHNM Oncology and Chemotherapy Wards
UHNM Critical Care Surgery Ward

Thank you also to the community teams who helped Jay when he wished to stay at home, in particular:

Douglas Macmillan Hospice – Palliative Community Care Team

Midland Partnership Foundation NHS Trust – Community District Nursing Team

Foreword

I was married to my best friend and soulmate for twelve years before he was diagnosed with Stage 4 Gastro-Oesophageal Cancer on 24 June 2018. He underwent Chemotherapy, a total gastrectomy, splenectomy and then further Chemotherapy and Radiotherapy. He did initially beat the Cancer but failed to thrive after his treatment, after six months and further investigations, he was given a terminal diagnosis of Peritoneal Cancer on 9 July 2019. He passed away peacefully at home holding my hand on 25 July 2019.

This is my uncensored real-life journey of caring for someone with cancer and also my experiences of bereavement and grief. It is written using real thoughts and feelings and based on factual events, it provides a raw insight into the pure emotions experienced on a day-to-day basis and how ultimately, I used those experiences to forge my way through bereavement and onto an inspirational journey of finding hope, encouragement and a renewed lust for life.

If you are going through a similar situation, I hope this book will help you to realise that you are not alone and that the thoughts and feelings you go through are very real. I also hope it shows that despite the darkest of days it is possible to remember the ones we lose with courage and a determination to turn something so difficult into a life of purpose and hope.

However, you read this book whether you be a carer yourself, a family member, a friend or a medical professional it can offer a profoundly inspiring and unique insight from a side of the journey you may not be aware of.

Chapter 1

Sunday 24 July 2019 and I am sitting in the waiting room of the Endoscopy suite at the hospital, I am waiting for Jay to be called through for his procedure. Small talk is the only talk but I'm trying to think positive so that I don't make Jay more nervous than he already is which is hard given that pretty much all of the posters and leaflets within the unit are related to Cancer. The waiting room is simple but effective, rows of plastic chairs fill a large space and there are a handful of other patients in the waiting room all looking equally nervous.

After what felt like hours but was only in reality ten-fifteen minutes, Jay was called through; I said my goodbyes and headed off to the hospital cafe, for the answer to all life's problems, a cup of tea. I sat observing the people coming in and out of the hospital entrance wondering what their story was, were they having treatment, visiting a patient or a member of hospital staff. It's very easy to assume that if someone is smiling that they are happy, we just don't know what that person is going through, they could have just received the best or worst news of their life but everyone else around them is going about their business in the normal daily routine.

I paused and took time to think about what could be happening to Jay and how he was feeling, I knew he was scared, he had told me that and he was nervous about the procedure but we were both very resilient and as long as we were together, we felt like we could overcome any obstacle thrown our way.

Of course, I had been on the internet to find out what an Endoscopy procedure entailed and apart from the uncomfortable feeling it seemed quite safe, so my mind was at ease in that sense.

Basically, the procedure involves a long tube that has a camera on the end which is carefully inserted via the mouth and down the throat to visualise the internal structures. The images are then used to provide a diagnosis for the patient. In Jay's case, it was to diagnose why he was having trouble swallowing and why he had a strange sensation of food getting stuck in his oesophagus.

Jay had otherwise been incredibly healthy; he played football every Sunday in a league and often played indoor football in the week too. He was a reasonable weight for his height and other than the swallowing problems, he had no other symptoms. He only went to see the Doctor as one night he nearly choked on a piece of food so he thought he would go just to see if he could get some better antacid type medication. We had already been reassured as he had also had a private medical check-up and all the tests had come back clear, so apart from that one symptom, we hadn't really thought anything bad at all.

He had visited the Doctor at our local surgery on the Thursday and the Doctor referred him there and then to the Endoscopy Unit at Stafford hospital, the appointment was made for three days later on the Sunday. Whilst we were a bit concerned that it was very quick, we tried to dismiss any bad thoughts and praised the NHS for such an amazing service. The thoughts about that day though were always on our mind, it may only have been three days but it felt like three weeks.

When we had arrived at the hospital that day we didn't know what the future held, we didn't really expect anything too bad and in general, we were positive that finally, he would be able to understand the reason for the swallowing issues.

I have never been a very religious person but whilst I sat waiting, I felt an overwhelming urge to be somewhere peaceful, not an easy thing in a busy hospital but I found myself walking towards the spiritual room. There I found rows of chairs, beautifully tailored in green velvet, the walls adorned with pictures of Jesus and the cross, along with beautiful flowers and greenery. As I made my way to the chairs, I sat down, all of a sudden, the busy corridors silenced and it was just me, in a room with my own thoughts and emotions.

The negative thoughts all of a sudden surged into my consciousness, the scary notion that it could be cancer or maybe a bad ulcer that needed surgery. My mind was racing with all manner of scenarios all of which led me to tears. I looked up at the stained-glass window which depicted a serene church scene. Breathe, he will be fine I thought. "Please lord let him be okay."

I sat in silence for nearly an hour without realising the time, until my mobile, burst into life. "Could you come back to Endoscopy? The consultant would like to talk to you and Jay together."

If everything was okay, they would have just said he was ready to go home but they didn't, they needed to see us, my anxiety jumped from high to off the scale. My whole body was shaking and I couldn't catch my breath. I had a sickening feeling which was unbearable and even though my body was walking in a straight line it felt as if I was dreaming. I have no idea how I walked to the unit, I don't think I can even remember it that well, I was just disorientated and fearful of the unknown.

Looking back now, I think deep down I had already suspected our life was about to change forever from the moment the Doctor referred him to the hospital. I was right. From that moment, life took a very different pathway, one which would change me and my life forever.

Chapter 2

Me and Jay had met thirteen years previously, after a few weeks talking to him online, we decided to meet up. That first meet up I remember feeling so queasy that I could hardly talk but the minute I saw him, it sounds really corny but I just knew that he was the man I would spend my life with. We sat on a bench near a canal in Stone on our lunch breaks from work, eating ice cream not knowing that that moment was to change our lives forever. It was love at first sight and immediately fell in love. After only six months we were engaged, and twelve months later, we were married (Only just mind but that's a story for later!).

There was never a moment in the twelve years that followed that we ever doubted our love for each other. Whilst we would have disagreements, we would never argue and we certainly would never go to bed without saying "I love you" and meaning it.

When I met Jay, he told me he had never wanted children but to be with me, he knew that I came with my two wonderful sons who at the time were four and six. It would be untrue to say that everything at first was a bed of roses but over the months/years, Jay loved the boys as his own and often referred to them as his sons rather than stepsons. The bond they shared and the love that grew was like something you read in a fairy-tale. Both the boys loved their biological dad but they regarded Jay as a father figure too. That wasn't to say there were no disagreements over the years when Jay's patience was tested by all the varying childhood traumas but he always made me smile when he spent time with them.

Jay was an avid football fan, in particular his beloved Manchester United, he had been a lifelong fan. He also played two/three times a week himself and was a much-loved player in several local teams over the years, I know that the teams who played with Jay would definitely say that he was 'spirited' as he definitely would never hold back with his opinion about a tackle or a referee's decision. Football was an incredibly important part of his life and from day one I was under no illusion that I had to learn to love football, with no exceptions. Fitness was also very important and Jay was a regular at the gym, especially in the weights section. He was so proud of his deadlift weight and would often remind me with a quirky little smile on his face. He met many of his amazing friends during his time at the gym, some of them becoming lifelong friends. He was blessed with many friends and enjoyed many holidays in his youth, with many a story being told about his antics which usually involved copious amounts of alcohol and mischievous behaviour but all in the very best of fun. His friends were always important to him, especially the group of friends affectionally known as the 'golden oldies' who are not necessarily old (birth age and the age think you are, is completely different guys!) but they are definitely worth their weight in gold as they remain to this day some of my closest friends who I love dearly.

We were married in 2008 but only just after our Registrar failed to arrive for the ceremony. After a couple of hours and more than a few phone calls we found a Registrar and 2.5hours late we were married. It's fair to say that no one will ever forget our wedding as it was definitely unusual but it was always about one thing and that was simply love and two people wishing to spend the rest of their lives together.

In the years, we spent together, we enjoyed countless holidays, with our favourite destination being the Caribbean, we went numerous times and loved every single holiday we had there.

I remember our honeymoon in particular, where we decided to do a Catamaran trip in Cuba; in theory that sounds perfect but I have a rather unusual phobia of fish, so going on a boat is a rather big deal for me but I was determined to go. All was good until they stopped the boat in the middle of the ocean and started handing out snorkelling gear; obviously, I was horrified and did thankfully manage to excuse myself, preferring to sunbathe on the deck.

The reason that day stays with me to this day is that that was the day Jay decided to lose his wedding ring to the Atlantic Ocean whilst snorkelling, something I never let him forget as he had only been wearing it for two weeks.

Chapter 3

Having received 'the call', I walked back to the Endoscopy suite. Anyone who has experienced waiting for health news, either themselves or for a loved one will recognise the feeling of utter dread which comes from the anticipation of waiting to be told results. The feeling of heaviness in the depths of your stomach and the queasy feeling cannot be ignored. You philosophise what might be said whilst having hope that it will be what you want to hear, in the space of maybe just a few minutes your brain processes about a hundred different scenarios, all of which include the saying "What if?"

The walk back was probably only a few metres but to me every step felt like a mile, it was possibly the hardest walk I have ever made as I knew deep down that life was about to change.

As I walked through the doors of the Endoscopy suite, I could see Jay was coming through the main ward doors opposite the entrance, his face was ashen. The expression I saw on his face will stay with me forever; I could see actual fear in his eyes. I had never seen Jay in that state of mind before, he was always such a stoic and resilient man, so I instantly knew something was terribly wrong.

We walked into the small office and sat down. A nurse joined us and at that point, it was obvious this wasn't going to be good news. "I'm just going to say it, Jay, we have found a tumour in your oesophagus on the junction of the stomach, it does look aggressive and it does fit with the symptoms you have been experiencing."

At that point, there are no words, no feelings and no tears, the only thing I can relate to is like an out of body experience when you just don't have anything in you to either describe or show how you are feeling.

They showed us the report which showed in more detail where the tumour was sitting and how big it was. The tumour was sitting on the junction at the Oesophageal junction, which is where the Oesophagus meets the stomach. It was indeed very extensive and although at that point we had no prior knowledge of this type of cancer, we knew it was serious just by its size and its location.

In that moment, as we had previously dreaded our lives changed forever. It was a pain like no other pain I had ever felt but it wasn't medical; it was an awful deep-down pain which comes from receiving terrible news. You see people being diagnosed with cancer in the media and on television programmes/adverts all the time but it's always 'someone else' but this time it was me and it was my husband. In that moment, my role changed from a wife to a carer of cancer.

Over the longest ten minutes of my life, the doctor and the nurse did their best to comfort Jay and to inform him of the next steps but our brains were numb. I remember trying to listen to the medical terminology they were saying as I knew it was important for me to understand but despite hearing the words, they made no sense and I couldn't comprehend what they were saying, I just heard one word: 'cancer'. My hands were shaking and Jay was crying but I knew my role now was to be strong for Jay, he needed me but, in my heart, and my mind I was falling apart. I wanted to run away and I wanted to hear them say it was just a simple issue that could be fixed, I wanted us to be a happy couple who had the rest of their lives to go on holidays and enjoy life.

My personality is one which I need to fully understand and to be receipt of all the facts; this was so out of my control and I had absolutely no idea what was happening or indeed going to happen, it was terrifying.

How do you deal with news like this, how can you begin to comprehend what you have been told? In the space of ten minutes, you have a hundred questions but no voice to ask them, it's scary and frightening and it's only when you start to breathe again that you eventually find your voice and slowly start to come to terms with what you have just experienced. As human beings, we have an innate feeling of flight or fight in extreme situations, in this situation it's hard to make sense of anything initially as your mind races to keep up with the events unfolding. I'd like to say that it's possible to take it all in but I just don't think that's possible.

So, what happens next? How on earth do you start to process the information you have just been given, my logical brain recognised every single word they were saying and yet it felt impossible to comprehend the magnitude of the diagnosis Jay had just received.

Although it was Jay's diagnosis, it really does feel like it's yours too, which I guess sounds strange but, in that moment, you instantly wish it was you and you instantly take on every emotion and feeling that the 'patient' is going through. I wanted it to be me, not him; I wanted to take away his pain and to let him be okay. However, there is a moment during this stage where your selfish side then suddenly thinks, "I don't want cancer, I'm glad it's not me", which results in feelings of guilt for being selfish and not caring.

There is nothing which can prepare you for this specific moment, in fact just writing about is hard as finding the words to describe the magnitude of emotions feels impossible.

The overwhelming cascade of emotion and Adrenaline to hit your body in those few moments is truly startling and is something that no TV advert or news story can ever convey in its true form. This is real life; this is the real journey of cancer.

Whilst I am a dedicated supporter of our amazing NHS, unfortunately, the staff who run the wards and departments do not have the time to sit with every single person when they receive a distressing diagnosis, however, the time that they do have they use to its full extent. The kindness and compassion shown however is extraordinary, in those few minutes every member of the team goes to the greatest of lengths to do everything within their remit to care.

On that day, part of me needed someone to simply put their arms around me, to offer me some form of comfort, I desperately needed someone to tell me that everything was going to be OK and that despite this awful news, life would be good again. In reality, the doctor needed to see the next patient and the nurse had a list of jobs which was exhaustive. The truth is that all doctors and nurses would love to have the time to sit with their patients and to help them come to terms with their diagnosis but in reality, this just cannot happen. I truly believe that the clinicians who deliver the news and subsequent prognosis of such illnesses are the true heroes of our NHS as although it is their job, it must be so hard to ignore the innate human being in them that feels emotions just like each and every one of us.

Walking out of the hospital after hearing the news felt surreal, just like the hours previously, people were busy walking in and out, going about their business but this time, I remember thinking 'how dare you go about your business, my husband has cancer'. Why was their life carrying on when it felt like ours had ended? It all seemed very unfair as I walked past people smiling and drinking their coffee, I wanted to be them, I wanted to be anyone but me at that moment in time.

We walked to the car, we got in and then just sat there, I just felt numb, I couldn't even cry even though I felt like my whole body needed to collapse onto the floor. The drive home was quiet; we didn't speak, after all, what could we say, how do you start a conversation when your husband has an aggressive life-threatening cancer. I don't remember any single part of that journey home, part of me wonders if I was even fit to drive, maybe I was on auto-pilot but what I do know is that those nine miles felt like ninety.

I wanted answers but we knew we had to wait to see the medical teams before we could even understand the plan. Not knowing was by far the hardest part and anyone going through a cancer diagnosis whether that be as a patient or carer will agree that having answers is often easier than the waiting as at least you can have a definitive thought process about everything.

At this point after diagnosis, it's like a 'no man's land' scenario; you have the diagnosis but you are left waiting so knowing how to feel and what to do is a complete mystery. Life was now this unknown world of uncertainness and fear. Every minute feels like an hour, every hour like a day and every day like a week, time really does stand still and everything else is just insignificant. Your brain tries to rationalise but ends up in a confused emotional state as you simply have no answers to the many questions.

My summary of that day with Jay was one of bewilderment and pure fear, in the room I remember the team talking to Jay but in my mind, there was an element that the team were not seeing me there, I felt surplus to a conversation which I needed to be part of but at the same time, Jay was the patient, it was his cancer and his information to be told. I wanted to ask questions but at the same time, I felt I couldn't as I wasn't the patient. In reality, this is far from the truth of how a consultant or nurse would want a family member to feel and I am aware that the involvement of the family is paramount, but it is how I felt on the day.

This two-way interaction is something I learnt to be in control of in later weeks/months, I would always make sure I took a pen and paper to each appointment and a list of questions so that I was prepared. Ultimately, Jay was the patient and his care was the principle focus however, I always wanted my involvement to be important too as I needed to understand what was happening and going to happen. My feelings were that if I understood the facts of the situation then I could better support Jay. Jay was the person with the cancer but as a couple we faced it together; that's a philosophy that we maintained throughout the journey.

As a carer this element of the journey is emotionally demanding and it is hard to comprehend at first, as a loved one as you feel quite alone in those first few weeks and processing the increasing amounts of information about the diagnosis is very overwhelming. I felt as if I didn't want to burden anyone else with my worries and fears as Jay was the most important person and it was Jay that needed the support. I didn't want to talk to Jay and the thought of talking to anyone else just filled me with a sense of failure as I knew I had to be strong, I couldn't show any weakness, however, I soon learnt that this couldn't last and to be able to support Jay I had to look after myself too.

Taking time out to gather your thoughts and reflect on a day's news or just reflect on the magnitude of emotions is incredibly important. By taking five-ten minutes out each day, I learnt to process all the information and make it more logical in my head, I then felt more prepared for what came next. It doesn't matter how you take that time, you can sit in a quiet room, take a shower or go for a walk, just anything that affords you the time to think and process your thoughts. I found keeping a notebook to hand helpful, I would write down any questions I had or any niggling thoughts that kept me awake at night. A nurse once told me that most patients feel guilty about turning up to an appointment with a list of questions but the reality is the complete opposite. The nurse explained that if they are asked questions, it means that the appointment has meaning and that the patient and their loved one leaves the appointment feeling more in control and more aware of the facts of their care, in fact, she actively encouraged us to always ask questions and come prepared to each and every appointment. So, me being me I purchased an A4 writing pad and proceeded to take it wherever I went which was always smiled at by the teams we met. I think in the course of the journey I actually brought three notepads as I had used them so much.

There is no question which is not important as if you need to ask it then it is obviously a piece of information you want and need to know. No question is a silly question!

Chapter 4

Following a diagnosis like cancer, you experience a whole new and difficult conundrum, how on earth do you tell your children that their parent has cancer? How do you begin to find the words without scaring them? At that time, my boys were aged seventeen and nineteen so there was no way I could sugar-coat the truth, they deserved to know the facts so they could be fully aware of the diagnosis. They needed the chance to find their own way of understanding and coming to terms with what had happened and what the future potentially looked like.

Walking through the front door on that initial day, we didn't know what to say and how to say it but we decided that they were at an age where we just had to be blunt and not 'flower' the details. Of course, this would be different if the children were younger where a gentler approach would be necessary. We sat the boys down and we explained that Jay had his test and that the team had found a malignant tumour, we explained exactly where it was and that at the moment, we didn't know the precise details or the exact prognosis and treatment plan but what we could say was that it was cancer.

Watching the boys start to cry broke me, the pain I had felt in the hospital had intensified to a level I cannot begin to describe. I am a person who likes to understand everything but this I could not explain, I had no answers to any of the questions they were asking and it was hard to see them so upset. To this day and in my whole life as a mum, I can honestly say that telling them that news that day broke my heart. As a mum you just want to shield your children from harm both physically and emotionally; your job is to protect them from all that is bad in this world, here I was giving them news which I knew would make them upset and there was absolutely nothing I said could say or do to make it any better. I remember just hugging them, I simply had no words.

Over the following hours, I managed to get through several phone calls to parents, close family and close friends, repeating the story again and again and hearing our closest family and friends cry with the shock and asking questions that I just didn't have the answers to. That afternoon/evening we had a steady stream of visitors to the house, it was simply exhausting, both physically and emotionally.

One of the words which dominated the conversations during the visits was 'Why?' Why did he get it? Why Jay? Why is it such an aggressive cancer? Why didn't we spot it earlier? Why did the previous medical not pick up on it…? So many whys…Trouble is no one had the answers. We tried to answer as best we could but we were as much in the dark as our friends and family, we just couldn't tell them anymore than what we had been told.

That night when everyone had left, we sat on the sofa, we looked at each other and we just cried into each other's arms for what felt like hours. All Jay could say was that he was sorry, he felt like he was letting me down, truth is, the only thing I was thinking was how do we beat this and how do I keep the love of my life alive. It was possibly the saddest night of my entire life.

Even though sleep was the last thing we thought possible, the adrenaline of the day and the sheer emotional tiredness meant that we did actually sleep which surprised us both. Waking up the next morning felt surreal, you lie there thinking 'was it just a nightmare' but then reality kicks in and you know that this is simply Day Zero and from here on in life as we know was going to change.

What made the diagnosis even crueller at that time was that just 24 days earlier we had moved into our new house. We had lived together for ten years but after nearly 18 months, we finally had a house that we had legally brought together. It was the happiest day of our lives (Apart from our wedding of course!). It was our dream home which as a new-build we had designed ourselves so it was truly 'our' home. At that point in my life, I can honestly say that I was so happy, I honestly thought life just couldn't get any better; I had the most wonderful husband, two amazing sons, family, friends and our beautiful brand-new home. I remember lying in bed in that first week after we moved thinking finally I had got to the point in my life where life was just so perfect, I was so happy.

Chapter 5

In the days that followed the diagnosis, we made a very common mistake that affects pretty much the whole population; we used an internet search engine to find information on the diagnosis. Whilst the internet is a fantastic source of information and can be incredibly helpful in understanding medical interventions and conditions it can also be the exact opposite. Upon browsing the internet, we found a whole variety of information explaining the prognosis of cancer and the mortality rates etc, this was not a good idea as it only fuelled the already heightened anxiety. As a person I have the need to understand facts and information, I need to know the what's, how's, when's and whys about a subject but in this instance, knowledge is a bad thing and wasn't at all helpful.

What I learnt is that you should only read the information on hospital/NHS websites or the accredited charitable websites. They offer the most up-to-date and relevant information on the whole spectrum of cancers and the information is written by people who really know what they are talking about.

It's hard to comprehend what a person feels when they are diagnosed with cancer. Whilst as Jay's wife, I was there to share his fears and his overwhelming feelings I know that my thoughts were different to those of Jay who was the one with the diagnosis. One day I remember sitting on the sofa and Jay suddenly sat upright and said, "I have cancer." He said it three or four times and I couldn't speak; I could only watch his beautiful face as it turned to fear and his eyes started to cry as he suddenly realised the gravity of his diagnosis.

It is hard to find the words to explain how you can look into the eyes of the person you love and hear no words but just see so much emotion and fear looking back at you. That day I looked into Jay's eyes and I carry that moment with me still, it is something which I will never un-see or forget. Sometimes you don't need to hear words, you see them and you don't need to do anything apart from offer a silent big hug.

Whilst there are many accredited websites with information and many booklets available via the hospitals etc what they cannot truly convey is the psychological impact of a diagnosis. Reading about emotions is completely different to actually experiencing them.

Over the next few days, we started to receive different letters and phone calls booking appointments for consultant appointments, scans, oncology appointments and blood tests.

In general, as a society, we are very quick to be negative about our NHS service, however, within two weeks we had had a diagnosis, a laparoscopy booked, an oncology appointment and a consultant's appointment booked; it was exactly what we needed as waiting is the worst part of any cancer diagnosis. We are so grateful to the NHS for this prompt response as it gave us optimism that we could actually deal with the cancer as soon as possible which gave us hope.

It was during this time that we found the strength to decide that although we were scared about the future, we were both determined to be positive and do everything within our remit to fight this cruel disease. Our negativity turned into a relentless and passionate determination to beat the big C. Jay's fighting spirit was inspiring, every part of him was broken-hearted but at the same time, he was determined to be a survivor and not a statistic. He wrote posts on his social media which were both moving and inspirational, the support he received due to this was overwhelming, he was spurred on by the support and to this day I don't think everyone really knows what a positive impact that had on not just Jay but myself, it was truly heart-warming.

We knew that the future was uncertain and we knew that the appointments would be relentless so before Jay had his PICC line (A semi-permanent treatment line inserted under the skin to deliver the chemotherapy drugs), we organised a romantic spa break for that weekend so we could make cherished memories before the treatment plan started.

Having that time away was incredibly important as it gave us the time, we both needed to process and take on board all of the information we had been given and to prepare ourselves mentally for the challenge that lay ahead; the calm before the storm as we called it at the time.

Chapter 6

That following week we started our journey, we had no idea what to expect, we were every kind of emotion you can imagine but the overriding one was definitely determination. That doesn't mean that we didn't have our moments or more to the point when I had my moments. Knowing the love of your life is seriously ill is overwhelming and at times, you find yourself not really knowing how to feel. Looking in his eyes, he was still my amazing husband but now he was my amazing husband who has cancer and that never seemed to leave me.

My heart was breaking but I knew that if I showed that emotion, I could potentially derail his willpower and courage, so if I needed to cry, I would simply sit in the shower with the door closed and fan on so that the running water would drown the tears, which were uncontrollable and heart-breaking at times. When the sadness had passed, I put on a smile and carried on. Looking back, I know that this probably wasn't the wisest decision to make, I was right to shield Jay from my sadness to a certain extent but at the same time, he later said that by offering me comfort it made him feel like my husband still and that he had purpose. I had never reflected on it like that before and I now realise that by having a purpose, it empowered him to carry on. I'm not going to lie, I still cried when I needed to but at the same time, I started to share that emotion so that I didn't have to carry all the burden of the emotion on my own.

The days and weeks that followed were really hard, every day felt like a week and every time the phone rang you were on edge thinking something was wrong. The familiar feeling of nausea and stomach churning which had become much too familiar was there every time the phone rang or we received another letter. I don't think that feeling ever went away and even now if I sit and think about it I can imagine that overwhelming feeling of trepidation.

Of course, throughout all this life was still ongoing; we both had jobs and we still had bills to pay so as much as life stops you have to also appreciate that it has to carry on. Thankfully, both our employers were incredibly supportive; we were both given initial compassionate leave to support us in coming to terms with the diagnosis and we were both offered a plethora of support which we both are so grateful for.

Waiting for that first oncology appointment was the slowest four days I think I have ever experienced. You desperately want the appointment so you can start to understand the process but at the same time, you dread it as you have no idea of the outcome and you know deep down that the news is going to be tough and that they are about to set you on a pathway of definite uncertainty.

When the appointment day arrives and you find yourself sitting in the waiting room of a hospital department no one wants ever wants to visit, the cancer care centre. A hundred questions are in your mind, so many why's, what's, when's etc. I held Jay's hand so tight he smiled at one point and told me that he would need a new hand too if I squeezed any harder, that laughter broke the silence which was a welcome change to the eerie quietness of the waiting room.

Looking around the room, there were numerous posters about cancer prevention and support services available, it reminded me of how real the situation actually was, this wasn't an episode in a TV drama or a story in a news bulletin, this was real life, this was our life, a life which we didn't choose but we had to go through, it was so unfair.

Being called into the consultant was just surreal; your brain is racing and your pulse is probably way too high to be healthy. You are terrified of what is about to happen but you have no choice but to hear it and let it happen. At this point, déjà vu sets in and all of a sudden, I am back in Endoscopy, I am walking through the doors and seeing Jay's ashen face, all of those physical feelings overwhelm my body and I instantly feel nauseous and dizzy. Life is about to change again; I am about to find out how I will be the carer of someone with cancer.

The appointment is dreamlike and you find yourself once again hearing the words but not really understanding them but within fifteen minutes, we had been told the treatment plan and what was going to happen over the forthcoming days and weeks.

All of my well-laid plans to listen carefully and make sure I took notes went out the window in that first meeting, it was just too much to take in, in such a short space of time. You try to pay attention to the meaning of the words being spoken but the saying that you only really hear what you want to hear is so true. This was a trait that I learnt to overcome over the coming weeks and months as I realised that the key to dealing with this journey was to breathe and then listen to the details, however I definitely cannot say that I was perfect at this as I still had my moments when I lost all sense of time, my hearing and my ability to comprehend simple words.

That short fifteen-minute-long appointment started a journey that would be life-changing not just for Jay but all those around him, including me.

In his treatment plan the first step was a Laparoscopy, a procedure to take a look inside his stomach to visualise the tumour in more detail and to take biopsies to formally grade the cancer. Once again, we were back to waiting for an appointment, however thankfully this time the appointment was incredibly quick, just two days.

Chapter 7

On the day of the Laparoscopy, we travelled to the hospital for 07:30 hrs so he could get settled on the day ward ready for the procedure. Once again that nauseous, heavy feeling consumed my body but I knew if I felt like that then Jay's anxiety was double that so I stoically put on a brave face to offer him assurance.

He was led to his bed and within a few moments, his consultant met us to talk us through the procedure. We were incredibly lucky to be under the care of a very well-respected consultant, Oesophagogastric Surgeon, not only was he an expert in his field but as a person, he was genuinely one of the warmest and kindest clinicians I have ever met, he always made us feel at ease and although being incredibly busy he made us feel that we were the only patient on his caseload. He talked us both through the procedure and what to expect recovery wise and explained that he would see us in his next clinic a week later to go through the results. For the first time since the diagnosis, we had a sense of hope, we knew that we had a journey still to go but finally we could see that maybe, just maybe Jay could beat it. This was until I had to leave Jay.

I had been quite stoic up to that point and with a sense of hope in my mind I walked out of the ward feeling okay however I then had a rush of unexpected emotion which simply broke me. I hid in a hospital toilet for over half an hour sobbing until someone knocked on the door to see if I was OK, it was just so overwhelming. The reality was that I could do nothing to help Jay, he was in the hands of an amazing team but as his wife there was just nothing I could do, I had no control over anything which was happening.

I knew I wasn't safe to drive home so I decided to stay at the hospital that day so I settled in for a long wait in the waiting room waiting for the call from the ward to say he could go home.

After two hours, to my surprise, I was called through to the ward. Jay was sat up in bed, feeling sore but I instantly recognised his emotions through his ashen face, I knew it wasn't just drowsiness, he looked scared. He explained that when he came around the consultant had said that he would speak to him on the ward but that he wanted me there too. That time sitting by his bed felt like the longest wait, we tried to talk but it was hard to know what to talk about as we both knew what was likely to happen, I needed to feel positive but my heart was breaking knowing that it was potentially bad news.

After an hour, the consultant arrived on the ward and asked us to follow him to a side room. What followed was one of the worse moments in my entire life.

The walk to the room was probably only a few steps away but I held his hand so tight. If that walk had been a few metres or a few miles I wouldn't have noticed, I was in a daze and full of emotion.

The consultant spoke calmly to us and explained that when they had looked inside, they had seen the tumour as expected, however, it was bigger than they had initially thought and more invasive into the actual lining of the stomach. He explained that the cancer had spread through the lining and was encroaching on the other organs but as far as they could see it had not spread to other organs, however, they had found a number of suspicious nodules on the peritoneal sac (The lining which surrounds the organs in the abdomen). The nodules were extensive and covered the whole area and in his professional opinion these nodules looked cancerous but he had taken biopsies to confirm the diagnosis and could not confirm that for definite until he had seen the results.

Through the stunned silence, Jay immediately asked the horrible question, "Is it terminal?"

The look of the consultant and the nurse in the room changed, the room suddenly went quiet, time stood still and then he simply nodded to indicate yes. He explained that in his opinion we were not looking at curative treatment but more palliative care options, however he still wanted to see the results first as he needed to know for sure.

It's hard to describe how you will react to the news that the love of your life is dying; up to now the determination and sheer stoicism had got me through to that point but it's very hard to find anything which is remotely helpful when faced with such devastating news.

Jay sat there with tears in his eyes and shakily grabbed my hand as he took in the information. I knew the consultant was talking still, something about the fact he needed the confirmation from the biopsies before he could suggest a palliative care plan but if I'm honest I didn't hear any of it and to this day, I could not tell you what was said.

He offered to give us some time and the Specialist Nurse stayed with us but then offered to give us a few moments together before we went back to the ward to be discharged.

We sat in complete silence until Jay started to cry uncontrollably, we then just held each other until we felt strong enough to walk out of the room and back to the ward, completely numb and with no idea on how to begin to comprehend the news.

When we were back at his bed all of sudden, I felt so weak, I made my excuses and told Jay I needed some water. I just about made it out into the corridor before I fell to my knees, I couldn't breathe, and I was shaking uncontrollably and just couldn't put two words together. I was taken into a room by the nurse who was just overwhelmingly kind; she sat with me, made me a drink and helped me breathe again. The sheer gravity of the day had caught up with me and my body and my mind just needed to stop and reset, it wasn't optional I needed to fall down in order to try to get back up again.

I would certainly like to acknowledge the nurse who helped me on that day; the ward was full of other patients and yet she stopped what she was doing in order to sit with me and offered the highest level of compassion. That simple act of kindness was phenomenal, even though I wasn't the patient, they treated me with so much respect and kindness that I was able to recover, gather myself and walk out of the room back to Jay. I think I did say thank you at the time but I don't think she really understood the impact she had on me and how much it meant to me. She gave me the courage to get back up again when every fibre in my body was telling me to collapse on the floor and give up.

Just like after the initial diagnosis we walked out of the hospital in a complete daze, however, this time was different, this time I was not walking out with a husband who had cancer, I was walking out with a husband who was dying from cancer, it was very surreal. Trying to describe the emotions at that time are very hard indeed, whilst I could try to offer some form of explanation, it really would not do it justice. What I can say is that it's like true physical pain but no analgesia can help it, no amount of medical intervention could begin to take it away. For anyone going through something like that I can now completely understand when they say, "It's just painful and it feels like real pain." There are no words to describe it, it simply hurts.

Jay stayed in the reception as we walked out so I could get the car from the car park as he was understandably sore from the surgery. I walked across the care park and decided to ring Jay's best friend, I just needed to talk to someone. The minute he answered I broke down in tears, I couldn't talk and I couldn't tell him what had happened, I simply broke. After a sea of tears I did manage to talk to him and I did find a way of bringing myself back to reality albeit with mascara down my face and blood shot eyes! I got in the car, I drove to the reception and I put on a brave face, I needed to be strong again, for Jay.

This experience was to be one of many I would go through over the coming months. Although Jay was the patient, the experience of the relative can often be unintentionally overshadowed. Whilst the care of the patient is paramount the role of their loved ones is also crucial in their ongoing treatment plan and experiences. As a carer I didn't experience the pain and feelings that he went through but I did see them, hear them and feel them on a compassionate level. If anything, it was more frustrating watching than going through it as there was nothing I could do, that was to become a familiar feeling pretty much every day of the journey. You have an innate need to comfort and to offer solace but at the same time, you have to protect your own mental health and appreciate that in order to be a carer you also have to care for yourself. I know that every fibre in my body wanted to support and help Jay but at the same time, if I let myself become overwhelmed then that support would not be to his full potential. There is no secret or magical piece of advice as to how to preserve your mental health after hearing such devastating news, it is unique to every single individual person, however, there is one thing that is effective. Breathe. Simply breathe, take it slow and take one thing at a time. Trying to climb a mountain is no good if you don't have the right equipment, so take your time to steady yourself, take a breath, ask for help if you need it, prepare yourself and then take each and every step, one by one. Is the above easy? Absolutely not, but it is true and it does help.

That following week, after telling all our family and friends the devastating news once again, we knew we had to find the strength to somehow adopt a positive outlook. We realised that if we couldn't beat cancer, we would try to outrun it. We made a list of what was important to both of us and then we spent the following week as a family creating memories and doing things, we enjoyed like day trips. We resolved to make the most of the time we had rather than spending our days worrying about the amount of time we didn't have. At times it was undeniably sad and we cried more than I can even begin to talk about. That pain I had felt when I had heard the diagnosis never left me, it was always there, some days being worse than others.

Then, about a week later, the most unimaginable phone call was received which totally changed our outlook. The phone call was from the consultants nursing team; they had the biopsy results back and wanted to see us both the following day. She was hesitant in telling us over the phone despite us repeating 'Why' many times but we sensed that it was good news rather than bad or why would they have asked to go in as how much worse than a terminal illness can you get!

Chapter 8

The night before the appointment we didn't sleep and the following morning, we arrived at the appointment an hour earlier than we needed to as we were so anxious about what they now had to tell us.

We were called into the office and as we sat down, he simply came straight out with the news. The nodules on the peritoneal cavity were not cancerous. He explained that it was the smallest of chances and that all of the team had not expected that result, they had all been shocked but at the same time absolutely delighted with the news. We had a lifeline!

It's fair to say that tissues were handed out to the whole room pretty much as we sat and cried happy tears, including the consultant and the nurse. I'm not particularly religious but I had spent every night praying that a miracle would happen and here we were sitting listening to a potential treatment plan instead of a palliative care plan. To this day, I cannot begin to put into words the feelings we experienced in that office, it was pure jubilation.

When the tears were dry and we had recovered from the news the reality of the situation was explained to us, which possibly did take the shine of our initial euphoria. The results confirmed the invasive nature of the tumour which had been officially graded as Stage 4 (the worst stage). The consultant very clearly and methodically explained to us that it was very aggressive and that any kind of treatment would be complex and that he could offer no assurances with regards to the prognosis. The ultimate goal was a cure but the cancer was so aggressive there were no guarantees. I just remember thinking any chance is still more than we had when we woke up that morning. I think we both just said do what you need to do, with no questions asked.

The plan was radical; it involved extensive scans, an initial course of Chemotherapy and then based on his response, the possibility of major surgery, this would then be followed up with more Chemotherapy and Radiotherapy if the surgery was successful. The plan would be intense, it was going to be hard but all we kept thinking was, it's a lifeline.

It was at this point where the reality of the new prognosis and situation really hit me, I had just spent eight days thinking my husband was dying and now here I was with a possibility that we could beat this horrible disease. My head felt heavy with way too many feelings and thoughts about the consequences of the treatment plan, it was incredibly daunting. I flipped from positive to negative thoughts and from scared to hopeful. I was understanding what he had said but at the same time I was asking myself to many 'What if's'.

Every day I would continue to browse the internet looking at the procedure, how it was completed, what the complications could be and what the average success rate was. I needed to know the finer details as it helped me to comprehend the enormity of the weeks and months ahead but once again, I was subjected to a lot of information that I probably didn't need to know and it just fuelled my anxiety.

The torrent of different feelings and emotions as a carer can be incredibly draining; it's easy to become overwhelmed, there's so much information to take on board which at times is very complex and detailed. The feelings associated with my husband were also overwhelming, my first thoughts were always with how he was feeling and how I could best support him, however once again this came at a cost to my own mental health. I started to experience panic attacks on an almost daily basis, they could happen at any time and had no real trigger, so whilst trying to be strong I was also experiencing quite the opposite.

In the coming months, I had to re-learn how to look after myself just as I had done in the beginning but it was a constant struggle to be both supportive and mindful of my own health, sometimes I won that battle, other times I was less successful but at all times, I did at least try to find a happy balance.

Chapter 9

In preparation for the Chemotherapy, it was recommended that a PICC line was inserted, this would allow the drugs to be given intravenously each time as well as being used for the regular blood tests that would be needed. A PICC line is a long thin flexible tube, it is put into a vein in the upper body, usually the arm or chest and can be left in longer than a normal cannula. Whilst this procedure is completely safe, common problems can be irritation of the insertion site and potential blood clots. Of course, Jay being Jay, he did indeed develop a small blood clot in his arm so the PICC line was removed and re-inserted in the other arm and he was subsequently given daily injections to dissolve the clot.

Over the following week, he also started to develop blisters and redness over the insertion site which turned out to be an allergy to the plasters being used to cover the line. This was easily solved by changing the type of plasters being used but was an extra source of anxiety for us both.

Only four weeks after the initial diagnosis, we arrived at the first chemotherapy session; it was quite surreal and not like anything I have ever experienced before. On walking into the ward, we had no idea what to expect. We were shown to a bay where there was a reclining chair for Jay and a chair for myself. Sitting down and looking around the ward, it was set out into sections with a nurse assigned to each area., It was notable though that every chair was occupied, so many people in the same situation and with the same fears as us.

It's a strange feeling sitting watching the person you love to be given cytotoxic drugs which you know will make them ill, you watch the various machines beeping and dripping the various drugs in minute by minute and hour by hour, it's very surreal. Whilst you know that the drugs are necessary to save or prolong their life, it's also incredibly hard as you wish there was more you could do but the truth is that you place their life in the hands of a ward full of nurses and doctors and their expert knowledge and care.

Even though the ward was incredibly busy the nurses were simply wonderful; there are many opinions about the state of the NHS and the levels of care but on a Chemotherapy ward, it really does show you the purest form of nursing excellence. Despite the unrelenting workload, every nurse would always have time to comfort an upset patient and they would always take their time to explain a procedure or drug so that both the patient and the carer understood what was happening, it really is quite humbling to watch and experience.

I decided to use the time wisely, by that I mean I listened to my music and occasionally watched TV on my tablet. It's the honest truth that despite the negative characteristics of

Chemo days, it was actually a day that I looked forward to, for one day a week I could relax knowing that he was in good hands both clinically and emotionally. I felt more relaxed on Chemo days than at any other time which was bizarre given the circumstances.

If I was to offer any advice to a carer in the same situation, I would simply say relax and use that time to switch off from everything, your loved one has a team of experts around them to immediately care for them if they are taken ill, use that support as it really does make a difference. I used to simply go and sit outside for a while with a drink and some food as I knew that I could be assured that Jay was safe and well looked after, I could have some time to myself knowing that I didn't have to worry. It's important to recognise that it's in no way selfish, it is simply self-preservation. Jay always used to encourage me to leave him on his own Chemo days as he knew how cathartic it was for me, in return, it made him feel happier as he always used to worry about being a burden so to give me that space was good for him too.

Post-Chemo day was always a good day as the steroids he was given gave him a boost, so for the two days after treatment life was normal (Within reason!). If anything, he would be on a bit of high and his sense of humour was really quite funny at times. I remember one day him laughing at a TV programme with proper belly laughs. In those moments all of the bad just went away and the sense of normality was wonderful for us all.

Like with most experiences with every high there may be a low and after that encouraging two days, he would then start to experience some of the common side-effects associated with Chemotherapy such as sickness and tiredness.

As the weeks go by, there is an accumulative effect and by the end of the cycles, the symptoms are often at their worse, however, they can be somewhat controlled with regular prescribed medication which is where the amazing specialist nurses' step in, they are able to listen, prescribe and monitor the side effects. It was about halfway through the treatment plan where the biggest symptom began to happen, hair loss. Hair loss is the most visual side effect of Chemotherapy and it is often the most emotional as your hair is often part of your unique personality. With Jay, at first, it was just the odd hair on the pillowcase but a week later, he could run his fingers through his hair and pull-out clumps so he decided that the hair loss would be on his terms. He retrieved the clippers and asked me to shave his hair off there and then which we did. Again, instead of letting the symptoms control him, he took control which was one of his endearing qualities, he never denied that he had cancer but he wasn't prepared to let it win at everything. Seeing him with no hair was a source of great hilarity for myself and our sons, rather than it be seen as a negative we would make jokes and giggle about it which looking back made a massive difference to what was a really life changing moment.

Walking into the Chemotherapy that following week with no hair, it was like he was proud, he instantly found his favourite nurse and showed off his new balding head, smiling constantly and making jokes about needing more winter hats.

By that time, we were accustomed to the routine of the Chemo days, we knew what to expect each time, which was comforting to us both. There was one particular day that sticks in my mind more than any other day, it started as a normal day, however, the nurse looking after Jay started to talk about a new song which was driving her kids mad, *Baby Shark*.

That day Nurse and I drove everyone mad with both our singing and actions which to us was funny but to everyone else must have been really quite annoying. I'm sure all the other patients did see the funny side of our antics in the beginning but after six hours, I have to admit to wondering if we were indeed making them ever so slightly exasperated.

Chapter 10

After the initial cycle of Chemotherapy, we had our first real scare with Jay's health. As part of the Chemotherapy programme, I had to take Jay's temperature every day to ensure that he was continuing to tolerate the regime. On this particular day, he had a really restless night; he was being constantly sick and was incredibly drowsy. By the afternoon of that day, I started to worry as he was beginning to slur his words and his temperature was up to 38.5°. After speaking with the emergency helpline, I was asked to take him to A&E.

On arrival, we were immediately placed in a side room due to him being immuno-compromised, by this point, Jay was hardly responding to me and even though I am quite stoic, I was genuinely concerned. After ruling out Sepsis, he was transferred up to a ward where he continued to violently vomit and become more disorientated. His temperature had risen to 39.5°, and there were doctors in and out of the room putting up drips and different medications, I had no idea what was happening and what they were treating him for, it was both frightening and distressing to watch. He was in and out of consciousness and he just wasn't improving at all.

It was around 02:00 hrs when the whole day just overwhelmed me.; I was sitting watching him finally sleep and I went into a full panic attack. Thankfully, a very kind nurse was walking past and came in to help me, I was helped to breathe out the attack and they kindly made me a hot drink and offered me some food. Once again, I was struck by the fact that despite it being the middle of the night and there being a full ward of patients that particular nurse sat with me until I was ready to go back to Jay. She took the time to ask me about Jay and his journey to that point and if I understood what was happening, she took the time to make sure I was aware of all the information in relation to Jay's treatment and what the plan was in relation to his care. By the end of that conversation and by taking the time to explain things to me, I felt stronger than I had done in weeks, she empowered me to keep going.

It was decided that Jay would be transferred to the local specialist cancer unit by ambulance in another hospital as they could offer him the specialist support, he needed. He subsequently spent a full week in the hospital recovering from what was suspected to be a Gastro bug which had been exacerbated by his lowered immune system.

As a carer to a person who is really ill you go into a state of autopilot, somehow you manage to maintain a non-stop life which includes fitting in work, shopping, childcare, eating, sleeping, and of course, visiting at every visiting time to make sure you are there as much as possible. Although somehow you do just carry on it is, without doubt, exhausting both physically and mentally. I seemed to constantly be on high alert but with little to no energy but I still kept going, I had not been eating and most days I would only have one meal a day as I tried to juggle all my other commitments. Again, I found myself having to force myself to stop and breathe and just take some time out to preserve my own physical and mental wellbeing. There was definitely a reoccurring of me not looking after myself and getting to a point of exhaustion before I realised, I needed to stop.

Chapter 11

After Chemotherapy, it is normal for further scans to be arranged to evaluate the effectiveness of the treatment, in Jay's case, the aim was always to shrink the tumour which would help him swallow better and also improve the overall chances of surgery being more successful. We had been warned at the initial consultations that the tumour was aggressive and a total eradication of the tumour following the chemotherapy would not be possible, however, a decrease in size and symptoms was the favourable outcome.

Waiting for the scan results I remember being more nervous than Jay although we were both still trying to be positive. When we were called in to see the consultant, he explained that the scans indicated that the tumour had not decreased in size but that on the positive side, it hadn't grown.

The consultant explained that based on the scan results he was willing to arrange the surgery to try to remove the tumour, however, he was keen to stress that the surgery would be lifesaving and without it, Jay would be looking at a life expectancy of a year if he was lucky. We appreciated the honesty of the consultant but it was also quite daunting to hear those words. Whilst we were grateful for any opportunity to extend his life, we were also faced with the realisation that this would be a difficult surgery and he was giving us no guarantees.

The surgery being proposed was called a Total Gastrectomy; it involves the complete removal of the stomach; the small intestine is then pulled up to join up to the oesophagus. Over time, the 'pipe' as we called it, would start to stretch slightly creating a little sunken pouch allowing him to eat again albeit very small portions, instead of larger meals. It was scary surgery but if it saved his life, anything was worth the chance. We were asked to go away and think about it but within seconds Jay agreed to the operation as he felt without it, he had no chance, with it, he had a small chance.

We were given information on the procedure and offered follow up phone calls with the specialist nurses to answer any questions which we had. Walking out of the hospital we both had a mind full of questions, we were a whole barrage of emotions which ranged from hope to fear; we had been given a lifeline but at the same time, the surgery was as serious as it gets and he could even potentially die on the operating table if his body could not cope with the radical intervention.

That night we sat together to read and digest all of the information we had been given and whilst his decision had been made, there were still elements of hesitation.

Throughout our time together, food had played a very big part in our relationship, we had always enjoyed eating out at lovely restaurants and a night out always involved food and drink. This surgery would mean that eating out would be possible but it would never be the same. Jay's food intake would be a fraction of what it was, he would eat little and often rather than the usual breakfast, lunch and dinner. The thought of the changes was intimidating but we had to remember the bigger picture, without it the truth is, he would die, this cancer was not going away and the decision really was out of our hands.

As a loved one supporting someone with cancer, it is inevitable that at some point you will be asked for your opinion or asked to make a difficult decision. When Jay asked me for my opinion on the surgery, it really was an impossible question to answer. Whilst it goes without saying, I didn't want him to die I was overwhelmed with the complexity of the surgery, the possible complications, the long recovery and the long-term lifestyle changes we faced. The answer was simple though, extending his life was non-negotiable but the thought of what faced us after the surgery was for me the worst part as I knew his recovery relied on me being strong and fully supporting him through some very tough weeks and months. Life as we knew it had gone and we had to accept that life would be very different and we would need to adapt to a 'new normal'.

Chapter 12

On a dark, cold Autumn morning, we walked into the hospital, down the familiar corridors towards the surgical ward, it was a walk we had done many times but this time I was unbelievably scared. I knew the risks but I also knew the reasons for going ahead. We had many discussions about the surgery and we knew that this was the only option but it made that day no less terrifying.

We entered the ward and he was shown to his bed, I was allowed to stay until the consultant visited to talk him through the day but I was asked to leave shortly after. His surgery would take place at midday and I was told to expect a call by late afternoon when he was in recovery.

Leaving him that day was one of the hardest days I have ever experienced. I kissed him and told him I loved him and walked out not knowing what the next 24 hours would bring. It's hard to begin to put the emotions from that day into words and to offer any reflection on how you deal with the fact you have left your loved one's life in someone else's hands, there was nothing at all I could do other than pray and wait for a phone call.

That day the minutes felt like hours and the hours felt like days. I was told to expect a phone call by about late afternoon, so after midday I was looking at my phone constantly willing it to ring to say he was OK, I waited and waited and by early evening the consultant called to say he had finished.

He was very guarded on the phone and despite me asking questions, he refused to really answer any direct questions, but Jay had survived the surgery and he was in recovery, he explained that he had experienced some complications but explained that he would talk to us in the coming days.

Despite him being in recovery, I immediately went up to the hospital, I wanted to be there when he was on the ward. Despite being told I couldn't see him until they deemed him fit enough. I finally got the call from the Unit very late that evening to say I could see him.

I arrived at the SCCU (Surgical Critical Care Unit) to see Jay in bed with multiple tubes and machines hooked up; the nurses explained that some were for drainage of the site, some were for pain relief and others were for other clinical use. I took a seat and held his hand gently waking him to alert him to the fact I was there. He opened his eyes and a tear fell from his eye as he realised he had survived and that I was there with him. He managed to talk to me and I explained what I had been told. He was able to recall going down and then waking up to hear nurses talking about a problem during surgery, he thought he had heard the word spleen but he wasn't sure. To be honest, regardless of the facts, I was just happy he was lying in front of me alive and telling me he loved me, at that moment in time, nothing else mattered.

My visiting came to end and I left Jay to rest and I made the very familiar walk back to the car park to home.

Despite being okay in the hospital, the inevitable comedown from having survived on adrenaline and multiple cups of tea for a considerable amount of time came to fruition. On the drive home that night, I had to pull over and I quite literally sobbed, it was an outpouring of overdue and built-up emotion which was a result of the realisation that he had made it through the surgery and he was still with us.

That night despite still being worried, I slept for the first time in weeks, my mind and body obviously needed to just stop. It's very easy to just 'keep on going' and to put others first, I know for myself it comes naturally and it's something I have no control over, however, there are times when my willpower and my body have simply disagreed with each other and I have to just stop what I was doing and admit that I can certainly try to be a superwoman but in reality, even superwomen need to sleep, eat and take time out.

The day after his surgery, I visited again and was greeted as I walked in by Jay looking a little bit brighter and the consultant by his bedside. He explained to us that the surgery was complicated and the cancer as they suspected was very aggressive and had encroached on the stomach wall into the surrounding tissue, the result being that they needed to remove the spleen due to the invasion of the cancer. They had also shaved his Pancreas slightly as it was slightly encroaching on that too. The surgery had taken six hours in total and had been attended by a number of consultants from his team due to the complications.

Knowing how perilous the surgery had been upset Jay and he was very emotional but feeling invigorated by a good night's sleep and a good cry I was able to absorb that emotion and reassured him he was going to be alright. The complexity of the surgery had tested the skills of the team of surgeons but their expertise and dedication had saved Jay's life and he found it hard to say thank you to the consultant as did I.

The enormity of the situation hit us both, all the emotions of feeling relief over him surviving, shock over the extent of the cancer, the realisation that he really could have died and more than anything that he now had a chance of beating cancer was at times very hard to really comprehend. The rollercoaster of emotions goes far beyond what you think you are capable of; it still astounds me how as human beings we can endure such pain both physiologically and psychologically but the power of love outshines it all and with support you can really get through most of life's ups and downs.

Each day I visited and noted his progress, it was slow but it was definitely good, he was sitting up more and starting to sip water which was really positive. Whilst the experience had been incredibly stressful, I do remember with a smile that we did have so many little moments where we just laughed so much. Looking back, I realise just how important those moments were and how they really did bring us both back to us as 'a couple' rather than patient and carer.

One of Jay's little traits was that he needed to sleep in complete silence, so sleeping in a busy critical illness ward was not really conducive to a good night's sleep. Every day when I went in, he would smile and tell me about his night and all the night's activities, he turned into quite the neighbourhood watch from his bed and every day he seemed to have a new story to tell. One of those stories made me laugh so much and to this day still makes me smile when I think about it.

As I arrived on the ward, I could see he was smiling and upon asking why he was so happy he told me to take a seat, I guess I was hoping that the smile was due to me walking in but Jay was never the most romantic of husbands. He began to tell me how the night before had been a lot quieter than the previous nights but that had caused him a problem. He had suddenly started to experience higher than usual levels of wind which he assumed were his insides settling into their new anatomical homes. He explained that he knew he needed to pass wind but with a combination of pain from his wound site and the fact it was so quiet, he was trying not to for fear of repercussions. Sadly, for Jay, this meant that when the inevitable did happen, the sound and extent of the built-up wind were both incredibly audible, this resulted in a ward full of patients laughing and Jay pretending to be asleep in a vain attempt to deny responsibility but on the positive side, he explained that he felt so much better and he then fell asleep for a full four hours and felt loads better for a good sleep. For the first time in a long time, I belly-laughed and smiled until my face hurt from the hilarity of his story, every moment of negativity just melted away and for the first time in months, I had my husband back.

Chapter 13

Being released from the hospital a week later was a big event and getting him home was a trauma in itself, he was still very sore from the surgery and the journey home was the slowest I've ever driven, he felt every pot hole and every corner on that trip but he was incredibly thankful and happy to be going home!

Prior to his discharge I had to attend appointments with the Dietician and the specialist nurses so that I could ensure he was getting the right nutrition and that he was on top of his pain relief. His diet was solely liquefied for four weeks so I went into overdrive making soups and dinners which were both soft and very small in size. The change in daily life and our whole lives was about to change totally and it was fair to say I found that very daunting but as with everything else, I was determined to rise to the challenge and do whatever I could do to provide the best possible support and care for Jay so that we could adapt as seamlessly as possible.

Although the various hospital and support teams are incredible at explaining everything, it is only when you get home that a realisation sets in, life is irreversibly different. I became a bit of a master at soup-making and even impressed myself with my ability to cook a half-decent meal which was the right consistency, the right texture and tasted palatable. Liquidising a roast dinner, however, didn't fare so well so that one ended up in the bin, as did quite a few of my attempts but it was always a source of laughter when I managed to make something which looked like something you would find in a field rather than a tasty lunch.

If anything, this experience taught me how to cook from scratch and actually how easy it is to make different meals that are full of nutritional benefits and not the preservative-laden ready-meals. To this day, I still don't buy ready meals, now I know how rewarding it is to do it myself.

I remember during those first few days and weeks, so many people telling me to sit down and take ten minutes break but I didn't see my support as anything other than love for my husband, yes, I was tired and yes it was overwhelming at times but there was never a point where I wanted to do anything other than care for him and be there to support him.

I have worked in a Health and Social Care field for years and although I have never been a carer myself up to that point, it actually became quite natural to me and I took on the role with no hesitation, nothing seemed to phase me.

Whilst I coped well with the caring of my husband, that doesn't mean to say it was easy. There was support on offer from the Community District Nurses and the support team from the hospital and I was never complacent that I would not need the help so their number was always kept close at hand in case I needed any clinical or emotional support. I had learnt that lesson the hard way so knew that asking for help was not a bad thing, it was good.

When going through any life-changing event, it is more than normal to experience symptoms like depression or anxiety, especially if that support is caring for a loved one through cancer treatment. What I have learnt is that you cannot go through this journey without being affected both physically and psychologically, whilst many could argue that carers should show no sign of weakness and be there for their loved ones, it is that very weakness that actually makes them stronger. To have a weakness means that you acknowledge the difficult situation you are in and when you appreciate that it can be a struggle, you are able to address those emotions and feelings so that it does become all-consuming.

I myself found many flaws in my daily regime, I lost weight due to forgetting to eat regularly and my panic attacks continued to cause me problems. In response, I started to make sure I ate regular meals and that I sought support for my emotional health, the combination of the two helped me to keep going, but I did still have my moments, despite the help and despite asking for support. I came to realise that this was normal but I found it annoying that I couldn't cope on my own as I often felt like I was a failure and in particular that I was failing Jay.

Chapter 14

By Christmas, we had settled into a good routine and Jay's appetite was returning as well as his ability to eat more solid food, he even managed a mini-Christmas dinner which was unexpected but just so wonderful to see. Christmas was a joyous time, earlier in the year, we didn't even think Jay would make it to Christmas but he did and being our first Christmas in our new house, it was incredibly special. Life was good, I was scared but I was also hopeful for the following year.

After the Christmas and New Year festivities, it was time to get serious again and we were once again sitting in the consultant's office talking about the next steps. The plan was Chemotherapy and Radiotherapy, however, this time it would be as a 'mop-up' treatment plan which basically meant that although the tumour had been removed the treatment was to ensure that any little remaining cancer cells were eradicated.

A week prior to the start of treatment, however, Jay became acutely unwell and was rushed into hospital again, his dysphasia (difficulty swallowing) had returned and he was struggling to eat and drink.

The last month had been relatively calm so to have this sudden deterioration of his health was incredibly worrying; I started to imagine all sorts of negative thoughts, mostly being that the cancer was back. He was ordered an urgent endoscopy to try to diagnose what was happening.

On the day of the procedure, I didn't leave the hospital, I was too scared, despite the fact I was tired, hadn't eaten and I could get no clear answers about what was wrong with him. As I sat once again in a hospital ward, I wondered what Jay might be thinking and if he could comprehend what was going on around him. As a carer and a loved one, I often wondered how I would feel if I were going through his experience, of course, it goes without saying that I never want to but it's one of the hardest things to fully appreciate. You can shower a person with empathy and offer the best support you can possibly give but it never seems enough, it is incredibly hard to communicate when you sit and really think about it. You see the person you love, in pain and suffering and every fibre in your body is screaming to know how to help, it's frustrating but you have to place your faith in the medical professionals who are trying to help.

After three days in the hospital, and after his Endoscopy, the consultant sat with us to explain that the Oesophagus looked healthy and that he could see no reason for the difficulties in swallowing, whilst this was a massive relief, it didn't offer us any reasons for the problems he was experiencing. We were advised to start the Chemotherapy and Radiotherapy as planned and review in a couple of weeks.

Chapter 15

Cancer is a cruel disease and anyone who has direct or indirect experience will tell you that nothing prepares you for the demands it places on you as a carer, both physically and psychologically.

During my journey as a carer, I remember having many people around me but at the same time, I felt incredibly alone, the only person I wanted to talk to was my husband but I felt guilty putting any sort of pressure on him as all of his energy should rightly be on his own wellbeing. In reality, it turns out, he had noticed and did actually want me to talk to him; he explained to me that his guilt was born from seeing me go through this journey and not being able to support me.

From that day on, I promised (once again) to be more honest with him and if I was finding something hard, I would tell him. Of course, I did mean what I promised but I think there was still an element of me that held back slightly as his worries felt non-comparable to mine.

A week later, we were once again sitting in the Chemotherapy unit, unlike the first round, we were less nervous as we knew what to expect, however, it didn't make it any less scary. Like previously, though we approached it with a sense of positivity and determination.

When sitting in a Chemotherapy unit, it is very hard not to look around at all the other patients; I often wondered what their story was, so one day I just started talking to someone. There was a lovely lady in her mid-fifties who was on her own, she had been dropped off in the morning but then that person left. I was making a drink for myself and Jay so I figured I would ask her if she would like me to make her one, after all, she was hooked up to the drips and although she could move around, it was difficult to carry a hot drink.

What followed was one of the most fascinating days I think I experienced in that unit. We spoke for over two hours about her life and her cancer journey, she was the most incredibly strong and inspirational lady. She had previously lost her husband to prostate cancer and a year after, he passed, she received a diagnosis of Bowel Cancer. Given that she had lost her husband, it would have been quite within her right to give up and not to try to fight the disease however she was adamant that she would be cured and continue to live her life as her late husband had wanted her to.

We spoke about her desire to travel and to visit all the countries she and her husband had wanted to visit but never got time. She had two grown up daughters who had their own families and although she loved seeing them and her grandchildren, she still wanted to experience life and all its nuances. During my time with that extraordinary lady, I laughed and I cried; her stoicism and positivity was unforgettable. She will never know this but she changed how

I view life, from that day, I decided that I would always try to appreciate life from a positive angle and although there would undoubtedly be negative experiences in my life, I would never lose hope. To this day, I remember her with such great fondness and I wish I knew how she was now and if she did achieve her goals to travel.

I left the Unit that day feeling a renewed sense of hope and feeling a warmth in my heart which I had not felt in a while; a complete stranger had the ability to change my whole perspective on how I was feeling.

Chapter 16

Post-surgery treatment side-effects were always going to be slightly different so we did expect them to be more intense, we were definitely right on that expectation. The weeks which followed were dominated by nausea and tiredness and this proved a hard combination with Jay's already diminished eating/food intake.

I tried to understand how Jay was feeling but I don't think I ever did; I really can't begin to understand how ill he must have felt at times and how that was affecting his mental health. Caring for someone with cancer can be hard as although you try to imagine and to almost feel what they are feeling unless you have been through that experience yourself, it is very hard to comprehend.

You do over time learn to recognise and understand the physical signs which indicate something is wrong and whilst words are used to communicate how a person is feeling, understanding body language and subtle cues are just as important. I quickly learnt how to interpret a sigh or a quieter mood and I often guessed when he was in pain and when he just needed a hug.

Sometimes a simple hug or a kind word is all a person needs; the medications and regimes help them physiologically but psychologically the feeling of a loved one simply being there is an incredibly strong medicine in itself. There were times when I know he felt so poorly but I also knew all he wanted was to be held and to be told I was there and everything was going to be okay. The honest truth was that I didn't know if it would be okay but, in those moments, he didn't need to hear my anxieties, he just needed to know he was loved and that whatever happened he wasn't alone.

In this modern era, we have access to the most technologically advanced treatments and state of the art equipment along with the dedicated and caring medical teams but in essence, sometimes that simple innate need for human love is all we need but simply a humble hug is a treatment in itself.

In the next phase of the treatment, it was to include having Chemotherapy and Radiotherapy simultaneously. Whilst we had experienced the Chemotherapy previously, the Radiotherapy was new so we were both a little anxious about what to expect.

It's a very strange experience in the Radiotherapy rooms; we would arrive at the appointment time, Jay would get dressed in the waiting room cubicles and then when called by the clinician, he would go into the treatment room, five minutes later, he would be out and be getting dressed again. The whole appointment could sometimes be as short as 15 minutes from start to finish, it was incredibly fast.

Unlike the Chemotherapy treatment plan, Radiotherapy is administered daily so it's quite a demanding time if you need to travel to each appointment; in our situation, we set up a rota with the family as this supported me to still attend work.

Every day it was like a military operation with everything being co-ordinated in a diary so I could ensure that every day Jay had a lift to and from the hospital; this in itself was a stressful exercise but when organised, it offered me more control and I was at least able to have some time to myself and to work more regular hours.

During our previous outpatient appointments, the Oncology team made it clear that having the two treatments at once can be incredibly hard physiologically on the body and it was clear after only a week that Jay was beginning to feel the effects of the various drugs/treatments ravaging his system.

I constantly kept reminding him of the driving force at that time, I would remind him that this treatment was prevention; this was to extend life and to prevent the cancer from returning. I tried to be positive but at times watching him was so distressing. You see the person you love going through this treatment and you desperately want to make them better but it is the treatment that is making them better which is making them sick. It's a very difficult process to go through as a carer as there is literally nothing you can do apart from being there to offer love and support. I often felt powerless, I had no control and no way of helping him with the symptoms, it is unbelievably hard to deal with having no control being one of the hardest aspects for me personally.

I knew that I could not make Jay feel better; I could only be there for him to be his support and to ensure that when he felt down, I was there to offer him love and kindness, however, watching your husband sob into your arms on a daily basis is heart-breaking.

There were times when he would plead for me to agree for him to stop the treatment but then he would change his mind as he wanted it to work so he could continue to be with me. This cycle continued day by day with him wanting the treatment but at the same time begging me to stop.

When you have a grown man on his knees, sobbing, begging you to make it stop, I cannot tell you the strength you need to find the words to even try to make it better. I would simply kneel down with him and hold him tight and tell him I was there and that I loved him, it wasn't much but it was all I had to offer him.

Those few weeks were possibly the hardest of the journey; it was both physically and emotionally exhausting for both of us. Jay was constantly tired from the treatment and from the lack of nutrition and hydration. His weight plummeted and I could see that he was struggling both physically and psychologically. Whilst trying to support Jay, I struggled to find a routine to ensure I ate regular meals and slept regularly as I was constantly on guard in case, he needed me so my own health once again started to suffer too.

Throughout those weeks, it was beyond hard but I never once thought about giving up. My love for Jay was so strong that no matter what happened and how many times I felt like falling, I would stay by his side. Having that strong sense of love was what got us both through the tough times; it was our resilience and determination not to allow cancer to affect us that made us closer.

It was at this time that we decided to renew our wedding vows; it was our way of reaffirming our love and strength as a couple. We decided on November as that was the month we had got engaged. During those tough weeks, we now had something to focus on so when times were hard, we would sit down and start planning the ceremony and the party, it kept us focused on the future rather than the present which at the time was important.

In the midst of feeling so ill, Jay would often refer to how lucky he felt. Every night despite his pain levels or discomfort, he would always find the strength to tell me how much he loved me and to try to give me a hug. I never stopped loving hearing those words every day, it made everything seem okay for those few moments in time, it is a memory I will treasure for the rest of my life. It was a moment in time that was so simple but those are the times we hold in our hearts forever; those little moments prove to be big memories.

Chapter 17

What we sometimes forget is that although 'Cancer' dominates pretty much every moment of daily life, during those treatment months you don't ever stop being you.

At times, it's hard to remember life before cancer; you forget what your previous life was like and what the term 'normal' really meant. Our brains are wonderful biological organs; they allow us to feel every emotion, love, warmth, affection and a sense of belonging to name just a few. Those feelings allow us to get up in the morning and face each day with a sense of happiness and hope, however, as soon as cancer is a part of your life it starts a war with your rationality and confidence, irrespective of how strong you are.

In the beginning, when you first hear your partner has cancer your mind is racing at a 100 mph and all those lovely feelings metaphorically fall into a hole of despair, you think that they are a memory and that they are no longer part of your life. When Jay was first diagnosed, I remember feeling as if life was over; the love of my life was going to die and I was going to be alone and nothing I heard made any difference to the fact I thought life as I knew it was over.

During those first uncertain days, weeks, month's life, it's true, life is very uncertain; I remember saying to someone that 'my brain felt like it was full of bees'. What I meant by that was that it was just a mass of noise and I couldn't figure anything out, nothing made sense to me anymore.

In time, however, the noise lessens and you start to take control of your own mind, you start to process the ever-increasing amounts of information and start to make sense of the treatments and the physical and emotional changes happening on a daily basis.

It's at this point that as a wife/husband/partner you start to gain a sense of control and start to figure out a way of dealing with the mountain ahead of you. Now, I would certainly be lying if I said it wasn't a mountain to climb when you start to process everything, I was petrified of what lay ahead but I did start to compartmentalise my life a little bit better and I started to process all of the information so that it made more sense and had more logic in my head.

It was mid-February and after two weeks of Radiotherapy, IV Chemotherapy and daily Chemo tablets Jay was a broken man; I remember him crying in my lap literally begging me to make things better and to stop it all. He was that desperate one night that he asked me to leave him alone with his pills so that he could take control of his life and end the suffering. It broke my heart but my response was to take a deep breath, calm him down and allow him to gain his composure, which after a while he did. I couldn't make things better for him and I couldn't take away his suffering, all I could do is listen, be there and allow him the time to work through his anxieties. Normally, when he had 'a moment', I would just stop what I was doing and focus on him, I would simply wait until he felt better, no matter how long that took, night or day.

The thought never entered my mind that I would or could help him end his life, but after everything Jay had been through and was still going through, I would be lying if I said I didn't understand his reasons. He was desperate, in pain, tired and had no idea how to even begin to contemplate feeling better at that moment in time. There have been many legal cases in the news over the years of people campaigning about assisted suicide and euthanasia and I have to admit that I find it hard to dispel them and say I don't understand as the truth is I do actually see their point of view. I am sure that in years to come there will be further legal cases brought to the courts and I for one will be interested to see if the law will change in the future.

After a low day or week, eventually Jay would start to regain his composure and he would talk about counting down the days until it finished. The low moods however were not isolated incidents, they were a daily occurrence. As a carer you go into a state of autopilot on those bad days as your focus is solely on that person's wellbeing but after a while, it can become emotionally exhausting. My only advice at those times would be to focus on the important things and put anything else on hold so that your own mental wellbeing is protected and you can find the strength to continue to offer that unwavering support. It's incredibly hard and I cannot begin to put into words how I got through some of those days,

I wish I could write a list of helpful hints and tips but the truth is, I have no idea, I just know I did it.

We both always managed to find humour in our conversations and it was at these most difficult times that this came into its own. The jokes were often very dark but between us we understood the context. A good example of this is one day Jay asked me to make him a coffee but my response was "Why? Do your arms have cancer now, kitchen is through there, you lazy sod." Now, in context we were both giggling and Jay's smile was more than worth the comedy but to anyone else in the room, I am sure they would have been horrified at my response. For the record, I did go and make him a coffee, on that occasion.

Jay's strength during that time was extraordinary and I was in awe of his sheer determination to finish the treatment despite clearly feeling very unwell. He battled through the remaining three weeks and we went through the same ritual every day of him wanting to stop the treatment and give up but each day he would wake up and we would arrive at his next treatment session.

Being the voice of reason when times are tough, it is hard but if you can find the inner strength to be strong, the rewards are many. I chose to focus on the little wins as the smallest little positive outcomes feel like you have won the lottery and that feeling is what gets you through each day. To this day, I can still feel that warm feeling of joy and happiness when something went right or we had some good news, it's indescribable.

On the final day of Radiotherapy, I took the day off work and proudly accompanied Jay to the hospital. The end was in sight, he had done it and although very weak and very emotional, he was still here and had survived. As we walked into the ward the feelings were overwhelming. Jay started crying as we sat down and simply said the words "I did it babe", to which I responded with a big smile and a "yes you did". It had taken nearly nine months, two courses of chemotherapy, a life-changing surgery to remove his stomach and his spleen, a course of radiotherapy and more stays in hospital than I could begin to remember but from here on in, it was about recovery and gaining his strength again.

I remember that day coming home and saying I needed a shower, I didn't, I just needed to cry. The emotions were overwhelming; it was a mixture of joy, happiness, exhaustion and relief.

That level of emotion is hard to put into words but that night, however, we lay in bed and we both just cried into each other's arms, it was a defining moment and one which I will never forget; we both had a sense of accomplishment and a proud feeling almost that as a couple we had weathered the storm together, he had beaten cancer and our love was stronger than ever before. For the first time in a while, I felt incredibly lucky, my life was good and had meaning again.

When you love someone, you cannot imagine life without them, it's a feeling unlike no other. There is a poem called Captain Corelli's Mandolin and it is so perfect, it talks of love being deep like roots of a tree, which grow together and become one. This poem formed part of our wedding and our planned renewal and to this day, is still very poignant to me. When I said 'I love you' to Jay, I meant it with every cell in my body, I just could not imagine my life without him.

Chapter 18

Despite finishing treatment, it does take a long time to fully get over the effects, it's not like you finish the treatment and go back to normal life straight away, if only that was true.

Over the next couple of months, life was hard, what was supposed to be the end of the long road didn't seem to be ending, instead of getting easier, I found it increasingly difficult to see Jay struggling to get any better. The acute sickness, chronic nausea and weight loss continued to be a problem but now he also had a very painful back which at times would put him in tears. He was losing weight on a weekly basis and at that point, he was only 60kg, to put that in context, pre-surgery just five months previous, he was just over 90kg.

During this time, I questioned everything, maybe we had missed something? Maybe the cancer was back? Follow up scans and appointments failed to address why he was failing to improve, there were no obvious signs of cancer and no indications in any of his tests, which was good news but also incredibly frustrating as we had no answers to his problems.

As a carer all you want to do is help and provide comfort but I was unable to do that and I became increasingly upset with having no answers, I would often become angry that I couldn't help and unfortunately at times, I did take that out on Jay. I never thought he wasn't ill but I just couldn't understand what was causing him to deteriorate on a daily and weekly basis. His failure to thrive was happening in front of me at a speed I couldn't comprehend and we were becoming desperate for someone to find the problem and give us a solution.

In an attempt to try to take his mind off the pain and lift his spirits, we booked a short break away in a beautiful cottage in Lincoln; the aim being to relax and spend some time with our best friends who lived close by.

Whilst at times it was just what we both needed, after two days, Jay's pain was becoming unbearable and I had to ring the GP and hospital to get advice on how to help him. On the Wednesday night that week, he was almost delirious with the pain and the constant vomiting, he could not settle at all, so we decided to leave and come home so he could be prescribed stronger medications.

It was at this time that I, more than Jay, started to suspect that the cancer although not present in the scans, was back or indeed if had always been there in an invisible form. Whilst I am not a medical professional, I do understand the clinical information we were being given but I didn't need a Doctorate to understand that something wasn't right.

The range of symptoms he was experiencing and the fact there was no obvious cancer tumours made me query if it was possibly a secondary cancer but his consultant was doing all he could do to try to find the cause of Jay's deteriorating health and to offer some form of diagnosis and treatment plan. I trusted the team implicitly and I knew they were doing everything in their power to help him.

Looking back, this is when I truly realised that Jay was far from okay and that I had to be realistic that his cancer was likely to return and eventually, it may overtake his frail body. Never once did I say that out loud but I had a very strong intuitive feeling that I was right, but of course, I had to have hope and I continued to focus on doing whatever I could do to make Jay as comfortable as possible.

We were desperate for answers and the consultant agreed to admit him to the hospital so they could do more scans and another Endoscopy to see if they could find anything which would help diagnose the issues.

His weight was continuing to plummet, he had lost another 10kg in just a month and he was now unable to eat or drink to adequately support his own nutritional needs so it was at this time that he was offered a nasal feeding tube to help to keep up his nutrition.

While in the hospital, I was shown how to administer the feed and change all the associated bottles and tubes so that when he was discharged, I could take over his care at home. I listened so intently knowing that it would be my responsibility to care for him when the teams were not there to support him. Never once did I question not helping him but at the same time, I was conscious that it was going to be hard work as I was already trying to balance caring for Jay, working full time, being a mum and looking after our home.

It did indeed prove to be hard work but I quickly fell into a routine and I became quite the pro at cleaning and changing the feeding equipment and making sure that he was comfortable.

It wasn't all plain sailing though as the tube would often block or start beeping at all times of the night and day, this meant clearing the tube and making sure there were no kinks which was the usual reason for the alarm sounding. I became increasingly tired from the broken sleep and found it hard to concentrate at work as I was constantly calling and texting him to make sure he was well.

Despite having the feeding tube, he was continuing to vomit multiple times per day and that led to the tube dislodging and me having to often physically pull the tube out from his nose/mouth to stop him choking, this happened on three separate occasions. Watching him choke and the frightened look on his face was so traumatic but I was always calm and dealt with each incident as it happens, I went into auto-pilot, something I am still proud of but at the same time it was incredibly scary.

Those few weeks were distressing for us all and no one really can understand what that feels like unless you live it 24/7. As a carer you develop resilience to the distressing symptoms of the disease and you almost go into a nursing mode, you switch off the emotions and go about cleaning up vomit and other spillages without a second thought. I was always on edge but I accepted that and I was just happy that I could take care of him, it wasn't a chore, it was a privilege.

It is only when you have a quiet moment and you are reminded that the person you are caring for is your world and the person you love and that's when it's hard and hits you when you least expect it.

Chapter 19

After all the relevant scans, he was booked in for another explorative Endoscopy procedure on 9 July. I remember being so anxious and feeling so helpless as once again everything was out of my control.

At this point, Jay was well under 50kg in weight and was so thin that you could see his bones all over his body; he was malnourished and was surviving on sips of water and the odd ice lolly. It was hard to see him suffer and watching him struggle to even get up the stairs, he wasn't living at this point, it was simply surviving.

On the morning of the 9th, we arrived at the hospital, we did the familiar walk down the ward and he went through to his bed; I chose to leave that day as I knew sitting, waiting would just make me more upset, so I left for home. Forty minutes later, just as I was near home, the hospital rang, the consultant wanted to talk to us both together and could I return immediately.

It's hard to put into words how I felt after ending that call, my heart was beating so fast and I couldn't think clearly. Everything in my intuition was telling me that when arriving at the hospital, the news would be life changing, I didn't know why at that time but I just had the most awful gut feeling. Jay was texting me as I drove back, saying he was scared and that he needed me; that drive was the longest I have ever driven, I have no idea how I got there safe as my mind was certainly not focused. As I walked down the corridors, my heart was still beating so fast that I could barely catch my breath, the nausea was unbearable and my hands were cold and shaking uncontrollably.

Walking into the ward, I saw Jay and his face was ashen, he was already pale due to his health but I have never seen any person in my life look so scared. I was terrified too but I knew I had to be strong so I put on my mask and stayed positive but inside I was petrified.

Unless you have been in this situation you will not know that in most wards, there is a room and that room is a room where the hospital teams will take you to deliver bad news. It is a room off the ward with comfy armchairs, multiple boxes of tissues and calming décor. We walked together and followed the consultant and nurse into that room.

What followed was indeed life-changing just as I had feared. The consultant and nurse sat by us and I remember their faces being so sad. They had both invested so much time in trying to help Jay and to give him the best possible outcome to his cancer diagnosis. They had gone above and beyond to support not just Jay but myself too, they treated us like we were their only patients and it felt personal rather than just being a hospital number.

The consultant was never one to beat around the bush so he just said the words straight to us. The cancer was back, this time in his peritoneal cavity (As I had once suspected), it was aggressive and it was incurable. There was a silence in the room and at first no one could speak, we just sat looking at each other. I could see a tear in the eye of the nurse and the emotion on the consultant's face and I remember thinking that this must be the absolute worst part of their job. Jay broke the silence with a very simple question. "How long?" Quietly, the consultant answered, "weeks".

Jay looked at me and then just collapsed into my arms crying. Inside I was hurting so much but I needed to be strong for him, I needed to be there for him but the news felt like it could stop my heart, I couldn't breathe and my body just writhed in a physical pain.

After 5-10 minutes I asked to leave the room for a moment and outside the room, I quite literally broke, I fell to the floor and into the hands of the nurse who was already there to catch me as my body collapsed. My legs could no longer hold me and my body felt weak, I wanted to scream and cry but I was aware that Jay was in the room and I was also conscious of the other patients and the other staff on the ward. She held me so tight and said nothing, we just stood there until I caught my breath; he calmed me down and I went back in. The consultant and nurse then left the room so we could have some time to take it all in.

There we sat together on our own just trying to comprehend what we had been told but how can you comprehend it, how on earth do you deal with the fact your husband is going to die and in a matter of weeks?

How you deal with bad news is unique to every person and the fact is, there is no right or wrong answer. Whether you break down and cry, sit quietly or shout, it really doesn't matter as there is one thing that is the same for everyone, it's heart-breaking.

We left the hospital to go home but once again like all the journeys which had preceded that day the drive felt surreal and I have no idea how I drove safely. Pulling onto the drive my mind was at 100 mph thinking about who we need to call and how we tell people. It was just too much and for the first time in my life, I was out of my depth and I had no idea what to do.

Our first and most heart-breaking job was to tell our boys, how I didn't know but I chose to just be truthful as they were old enough to know the prognosis. Jay had been in their lives since they were young and he was their dad. We sat them down and simply told then the truth, the pain in their eyes is something I will never get over, it was truly awful and one of the worst things I have ever had to do in my entire life. I was broken and in one conversation I felt I had broken both of my boys as well, it was truly the worst feeling as a parent, knowing I had delivered such bad news and I couldn't make them feel better.

There is no right way or wrong way with regards to telling children bad news, I think as a parent you know the personality of your children and you know how to gage the conversation but whatever you say it still doesn't make it any easier. The boys were at an age where honesty was the only way to tell them, however, with younger children I think maybe I would still be honest but I would choose my words carefully in order to help them process the information.

After telling the boys we then had to tell all the family and friends and that in itself is so draining, both physically and emotionally, like the night when we had received the first diagnosis that night, I didn't expect to sleep but I did as I think my body was so overwhelmed by the events of the day I just needed to stop.

Chapter 20

Those following couple of days were a blur; they involved meeting the palliative teams from the local hospice and back-to-back visits from family and friends.

On that first day, however, we both sat down to start talking about 'the future'. I asked Jay if there was anything he wanted to do specifically and he replied straightaway to say that he still wanted to renew our wedding vows which had originally been booked for November.

In between the palliative care team visits and family and friends visiting constantly, I managed to arrange a renewal service for that Sunday (four days' notice). With the help of our amazing friends and many phone calls, I managed to pull it together so that we could at least have our special day.

By that Sunday, I had sourced a room (our original wedding venue!), a dress, a suit, a photographer, flowers, hairdresser, food, drinks and all the decorations. Jay's best friend was to be the master of ceremonies and my uncle would read a poem. What should have been quite stressful was actually quite cathartic in that, it gave us something to focus on. Jay really enjoyed the fact that we could renew the vows and he would get to enjoy the day still.

On the renewal day, my main worry was Jay's pain levels, he was in so much pain and at this point was on regular Morphine to try to keep him comfortable, however, this wasn't working and he continued to struggle, he was however determined to get to the ceremony and enjoy our special day.

I had to help him dress that morning as his dexterity was now starting to be affected and he was very weak but the main issue was that the suit he was wearing was now too big and we had no time to buy another one so with the help of some safety pins and some clever sewing we managed to make it fit. He did, however, look so painfully thin that it was obvious how ill he was, no amount of clever sewing could hide that fact.

When we arrived, we were overwhelmed by how many of our family and friends had turned up, they were all dressed up which made us feel so special that they had made so much effort. It was however obvious to everyone how much Jay had changed and I could see a tear in the eye of many of our friends and family as they tried to make sense of Jay's dramatically thin and gaunt appearance.

Jay's face when he saw everyone however will stay with me forever, it just lit up and his smile was priceless. We posed for endless photos and although there were tears, it was so special to see so many of the people who loved Jay stand by his side.

He found the whole day incredibly hard and kept whispering to me how much pain he was in and that he needed to more pain medication. I kept topping him up on morphine which was kept close by just in case but the pain was so bad that the morphine wasn't really helping at all at this point. I gave him double doses of the morphine that day as he begged me to get him to the ceremony no matter what it took. I knew what I was doing but I also know that I needed him to get through the day, not for me but for him. This day was one of his last wishes and I needed to get him through it.

I kept my smile on but inside I remember feeling such overwhelming sadness to see the man I love being helped up a flight of stairs, he had no energy and every moment was making him wince but we made it and he walked into the room with a huge smile on his face. I smiled too but I knew that he was in pain but I also knew that he didn't want people to know how much so I had to act as if he was fine.

I cannot put into words the love in that room on that day, Jay sat on a stool while I stood next to him as his best friend spoke and the poem was read by my uncle. It was so emotional, there wasn't a dry eye in the house. When it came to our actual vows, he insisted that he stood so he could do it properly which meant the world to me given the level of pain he was in.

After the photos had been taken and the room was filled with people talking and laughing, Jay whispered that it was all too much and he needed to be taken home by a friend so he could rest. He looked so tired but at the same time he smiled through it and made sure I was the only one to know the immense pain he was in.

That day was so special and being able to have those precious moments are memories that I will treasure forever. The help we received to help us create that perfect day was astounding and I cannot begin to express my gratitude for everyone who helped us, it was a true act of human kindness and I am so humbled for every single person who attended and shared our special day.

What made that day even more special was that England went onto win the Cricket World Cup with the final hour being one of the best I've ever seen in a Cricket match. Seeing Jay's face as the final wicket fell will stay with me forever, it was magical, his smile was so big and he turned to me and just said, "The perfect end to the most perfect day, I love you." It's moments like that you treasure, they are priceless and the importance of those memories for the future is undeniably special.

In the days which followed his deterioration was daily and by Wednesday of that same week, he was bed-bound and unable to walk. The palliative care teams were now visiting twice daily and he was provided with medication via syringe drivers to offer more pain relief and to make him comfortable. His health was now critical as he could not keep any fluids down and when he did sip any drinks, he immediately vomited.

It was at this point we decided to accept a home-hospital bed so he could stay downstairs. This in itself was a defining moment but one which I welcomed as it was becoming hard to walk him to the downstairs bathroom, never mind upstairs to bed.

It is a hard and sobering reality when things like this happen, the seriousness of the situation becomes real and you know that by accepting the hospital bed you are accepting the reality of the terminal diagnosis and that their health is deteriorating.

Caring for someone who is near the end of life is challenging for many reasons, it is emotionally demanding but physically it can be exhausting too, there are no books and no leaflets to prepare you for those demands and they can at times be overwhelming. Knowing the person, you love is terminally ill changes your perspective on life, set routines are disregarded and you live life hour to hour and day by day.

One aspect I was not prepared for when caring for Jay was a conversation in relation to assisted suicide. He had mentioned wanting to end his life previously when he was having treatment but afterwards, he did change his mind, but approximately a week before he died, he spoke very calmly to me and explained that his pain and suffering was so unbearable that he wanted it to be over, so he asked me if would consider helping him end his life. He knew that his condition was life limiting and that at that time he probably only had a few days to live so he wanted to take control of his own life and do something on his terms. At the time I remember feeling very confused about what he had said and despite knowing it was wrong I struggled to comprehend what he was asking of me; I loved my Husband and did not want to upset him by flatly denying his wishes but at the same time I knew I couldn't do what he was asking.

In retrospect looking back I actually now understand why he asked me and I feel an overwhelming sense of respect for him that he felt he loved me enough to trust me with that question.

The right to choose whether you live or die is a debate which has its supporters and also its critics, it has been contended in the highest of UK courts for years with the outcome invariably being that if a person assists someone to take their own life, you can be convicted under criminal law. In the case of Jay, the outcome was that I did not agree to help him but instead I contacted the palliative care team and they increased his pain medication which made him more comfortable. Jay understood my reasons for not helping him but I know he was also hoping I would agree so that he didn't have suffer.

What I learnt up to that point was that you should never be afraid to ask questions, if you don't understand something, ask. By speaking with the relevant teams who were visiting, I was able to understand exactly what they were doing, why they were doing it and how it was helping Jay. It's crucial that everyone understands what is happening and what is likely to happen, especially when the end of life is near. You only get one chance and the worst thing that can happen is that you regret not doing something as you cannot get that time back. Ask, Ask, Ask!

Chapter 21

While he could still talk and was okay cognitively, we talked as much as we could, trying to put the practical matters in hand, like his work, money, the house etc.

The hardest conversations were around his wishes for me, the boys, his funeral and the future. At times talking was just emotionally draining; we should have been talking about our future, instead, I'm being told what I need to do when he dies.

His words to me were very powerful and he sternly told me that when he died, I was allowed to be sad and to cry but that I also had to be strong. Following that, I came up with the phrase 'I will break, and I will fall but I will get up and in time I will walk forward again'; those words being relevant to this very day.

He told me that despite my sadness, I need to think big and to follow my dreams, especially with regards to my career. He always knew I had potential and that I was holding myself back so he told me to embrace change and take a leap of faith in whatever direction life took me. At the time I did listen and agreed to his wishes but little was I to know at that point just how poignant those words would be for my future.

The love that we shared was so special and from the day we met we always knew that we were meant to be together, however, cancer had unfortunately made that impossible and as such he would not be there to love me forever as he had promised. He told me to be happy and not to feel guilty about moving on and even loving someone again, me being happy would make him eternally happy so I had to make him that promise on that day. This, of course, is easier said than done as when you love someone, you just don't flick a switch and turn that love off but knowing his wishes was important and since that day, it has actually been a source of comfort to me to know that we had talked about it.

The promise he made me say was that if I did meet someone that it had to be because they loved me and for who I was and that they accepted my past as well as my future as only that way would they realise what a complete pain in the backside I was! This of course was said with a very big grin on his face but to be fair, it's probably a fair statement! He wanted me to be happy and he said it would be a comfort to him to know that someone would be by my side to be there for me and love me as he had always loved me. It was incredibly hard to hear and even writing this is hard as I can remember the feelings, I had on the day we talked, it broke my heart.

What those few days taught me is that although death and dying is often a forbidden subject, to talk about it is also incredibly important. In those few days, Jay gave me the gift of insight and I was prepared for what was to come knowing that he had chosen and guided me towards my future. It's really sad and incredibly hard to talk about dying but it's important as afterwards that sense of comfort of knowing what a person wants and how they want their legacy to be is central to the grieving process.

Watching any person deteriorate in front of you is hard for anyone, however, watching your husband slowly dying and being so weak that he cannot lift his own head to sip water or clear his throat, that's hard.

It's strange though as no matter how hard it was, I never gave up, I started to provide his personal care but never once did I complain, it felt automatic to do it and I was just happy that I could offer him some form of comfort. I spent every moment with him and never left his side, I felt pride in making sure I gave him quality to his life and that he was always comfortable. Even when I was offered a night-time carer so I could get some sleep, I just couldn't leave him, it felt wrong but at the same time, I was incredibly tired and needed to rest. I did eventually accept help from the local community hospice team who kindly send a carer to sit with him overnight but I found it hard to switch off and found myself popping down every couple of hours anyway.

There are no books, websites or healthcare professionals who can prepare you for what you see and experience when your partner is dying. The support you get is amazing but it is impossible to really put into words the emotions you experience. I spent many, many hours just watching him sleep and many more crying when I was alone. When he was awake, he would be very restless and would thrash around a lot but without being able to talk, it was hard to know if this was due to him being in pain, being uncomfortable or just feeling frustrated.

As a carer and a partner, I would say this is the hardest part and it is an experience that is hard to put into words. If I were to be asked for advice about how to get through this particular time then all I can say is breathe and take it minute by minute and hour by hour. Keep in mind that it is the 'disease' or 'condition' which is causing the distressing behaviour and that inside the person you love is still there. See the person, not their condition/illness.

It was at this point that I realised Jay was dying, it had been only ten days since the renewal and his palliative care team were starting to prepare me as they knew he was deteriorating faster than they had expected. The consultant had originally said he had weeks to live but we were only two weeks after that conversation, it was too soon and although I knew it was going to happen, I felt unprepared.

We had many visits from the palliative team in those two weeks and many discussions about Jay's wishes, at each meeting they would discuss with us all of the relevant options open to Jay and how he was in control of his care. It was at this time that Jay decided to sign a DNAR (Do Not Attempt Resuscitate order) and also complete and sign an Advanced Directive.

He was aware his cancer was terminal and that any prolonging life-saving interventions would cause more pain and discomfort with no realistic benefit. He was of sound mind when he signed the form and the full consequences of his actions were explained to him and understood. Whilst upsetting I knew that Jay was at the centre of the decision-making process, it was his decision and I respected that, there was after all no medical miracle cure or chance of sudden improvement, his prognosis was poor and therefore the ability to prevent further pain and suffering was at the forefront of his decision.

I watched him sign away his life and tell the teams what to do when he was no longer able to care for himself, I cannot put into words how that actually felt, it was just too overwhelming, even though I agreed with it all.

Chapter 22

Over the next few days, we had many friends come to visit, it was really lovely to see so many people wanting to see him but it was so exhausting. Every visit was draining in the sense that you could see the pain in the eyes of people who knew that they were saying goodbye as he was at that point extremely poorly. However, we also smiled so much and properly laughed as his friends would each tell a different story to tell about the 'good ole days' of clubbing and partying when they were younger. Jay would sleep a lot but when he was engaged in a funny conversation you could almost see the 'old Jay' coming alive again, it was wonderful to see and hear.

One night, in particular, that week, I remember we had had upwards of ten plus visitors in one day and it was late evening by the time the last person left. We were both shattered so I climbed on the hospital bed, we put the TV on and we just fell asleep together. I remember waking up an hour or so later and for a few moments, life was back to how it used to be. I think those are the moments you treasure so don't ever feel guilty about the washing not being done or that the house needs cleaning, just focus on those treasured moments which are irreplaceable, the rest is really not important at all.

By the following morning, I took the decision to stop all visits and to only allow close family to visit as Jay was becoming unresponsive and his pain was increasingly becoming worse.

Jay was still my husband but the man I loved was now unable to move from his bed, he was semi-conscious and was now on two syringe drivers and a strong painkilling patch. His pain was under control but this meant he was not really lucid and was experiencing hallucinations. I would lie on his bed next to him and talk however his only response was to slightly squeeze my hand when he acknowledged what I was saying.

Like in the times before I found myself living on auto-pilot and adrenaline as I didn't know how else to carry on.

Thirteen days after being given the final diagnosis he would have hours where he was breathing but unresponsive. Talking to him now involved physically rousing him and raising your voice and physically turning his head to your eye level so he could see who was talking. He was unable to talk and he was often not responsive to squeezing my hand. I realised that time at this point was limited and I knew the end was near, so every minute was precious and I made sure I made them count.

It was at this point that my parents moved in to be with us so we were together as a family and able to care for Jay around the clock, night and day. Whilst really there was nothing anyone could do, their support was vital as it comforted me knowing that I could take a break and someone would be with him at all times, he was never left alone. I was also appreciative of being looked after myself as they were providing me with some much-needed hot meals and plenty of cups of tea which I had definitely missed. They were also supporting my boys while I sat with Jay which meant the world to me knowing that they were being supported.

When sitting with Jay in those last couple of days, I would talk to him and recall stories from our past and even though he couldn't respond, I knew he could hear me and knowing I was there was all that mattered. If I needed to rest I would, knowing that my parents were there to wake me if I was needed. We would play music and put on his favourite shows so he could hear them and we would crack jokes to see if we could raise a response. I remember one time it was just me and Jay in the front room, we had some music on and I jokingly whispered something rude in his ear about us dancing to that song a few years previously in a bar. To my surprise, he very faintly squeezed my hand, it wasn't much but knowing he had heard made me giggle so much and was just a wonderful moment to remember. The fun-loving, outgoing Jay I loved was still in there and he knew I was there, that was priceless.

Chapter 23

The 25 of July was the hottest day of the year, Jay was incredibly restless and agitated and was drifting in and out of consciousness all day so I never left him alone. He was now not responding to us at all and we were sure he was in pain as his heart rate was incredibly high. The palliative nurses were called to administer more pain relief which seemed to work as the agitation slowed and he seemed more comfortable.

I remember reading the notes that day that the nurse had written in his care plan, the words 'actively dying' were written very clearly that day.

At this point, you have a sense of grieving for the man I love even though he was still living. It's very strange, even when you know you are facing a loved one's terminal diagnosis and you think you understand, the reality is so different and the level of emotion when the time actually comes is beyond comprehension. I kept reading the words 'actively dying', they never changed but every time I read them the reality became more real.

It was early evening when I was called in from the kitchen by my parents to say Jay was breathing differently and that I should be with him. Over the next hour, he quietly slowed his breathing, his body relaxed and his gait changed completely. I watched as his skin changed colour and his eyes became glazed, I held his hand incredibly tight and continued to speak to him. I continued to talk to him and told him not to be scared and that he should not fight anymore, I told him that I loved him and that all the things he wanted me to do I would do and that me and the boys would be fine. I reassured him that he was safe and that he had those that loved him around him. I meant every word of course but I know in my mind I did want him to fight as I wanted him to live, I didn't want him to die, but I also knew that his life was now not in my control, he was tired and his body needed to rest. I was logical in my thinking but at the same time my heart was simply breaking.

My last words to him were "I love you but be at peace now Jay, it's time to rest". A few moments later, at 18:30 hrs, he quietly passed away, holding my hand as I sat next to him. It was very calm and he wasn't in any pain.

In that moment, my heart broke and the pain I felt, to this day I cannot describe, it was unbearable. My parents were there and after a few moments offered to give me some time with Jay on my own as they spoke to the boys. I closed his eyes and I put his hand back in mine. I wasn't in denial about him dying but for some reason I felt I need to lie with him.

I remember placing my head on his chest and listening, I heard nothing, his heart had stopped and his body was still.

I sat back up and looked at him and through the tears I said goodbye.

When I reunited with my boys I had no words, the pain on their faces and the redness in their eyes was unbearable. I just held them both so tight that I thought I might hurt them but I needed to feel close to them and I needed for them to know that I loved them.

To this day I cherish every single hug with my two boys, I hope they always know that I love them unconditionally. I have never been and will never be a completely perfect parent and I totally admit to not always getting things right but I am so proud of them both and I hope they know that they are my world and my greatest achievement in life and that I will always be there for them.

There are no words I could write or any advice on how to deal with things in that moment, apart from taking as much time as you need to sit and take it in. Say what you need to say, do what you need to do but never ever rush a single moment as those moments are precious and should be treasured. If you need to cry, then cry, if you need to sit quietly then take that time, do whatever feels right for you.

After taking the time to be with Jay I rang the palliative care team and the nurse promptly arrived to confirm Jay's death and lay him to rest. He had been quite adamant that he was to be buried in his Manchester United kit so the nurse kindly dressed him for us as per his wishes. She took away all the medical equipment and made him look so peaceful. When I went back into the room, he was no longer hooked up to syringe drivers, he was dressed and for the first time in weeks looked so peaceful, like he was just sleeping. The pain was gone and he could rest finally.

End of life care is a very unique and important aspect of health and social care and is often not given the kudos it deserves and yet I know that I remember every single detail of those last days; the care offered by the palliative teams, the advice I was given and the support I was offered, it stays with you.

In a strange way, I felt privileged to be with Jay at the end, he wanted me there with him and being able to hold his hand and for him to know he wasn't alone, provides me a huge sense of comfort.

I know that the kindness shown to Jay, myself and the boys was something which Jay himself found truly inspirational. To the friends and family who took the time to visit and to make him smile at such a sad time, I cannot put into words what that meant to Jay and myself. The kindness and love we were shown was extraordinary. I hope that being able to say goodbye gave you peace and that you know how much Jay especially appreciated it. To those that used social media to contact me and even those who I had never even met but were acquaintances via the schnauzer site we were members of part of Jay's football family, I thank each and every one of you for your kindness and support.

There is of course an opposite side to my story in that I now appreciate that some families do not get the opportunity to be there at the end of their loved one's life through a myriad of different reasons. It is sometimes not possible to be there at that actual time of passing, so this can be distressing as the opportunity to say goodbye is not there, however, it is important to remember that our loved one's physical presence is only part of the relationship, their spirit and love is just as significant. There is no right or wrong way to say goodbye, it's unique to every single person.

Whether it is a special poem, a special place or a candlelit service, it is important to find your own way of celebrating their life and saying goodbye in your own personal way.

In death, it is the act of kindness that can be important. In the Covid pandemic in particular, this was and still is more significant than ever, our amazing nurses and doctors took time to purely sit with those who needed that simple act of human kindness, holding the hands of our loved ones in their final moments as if they were their own. To the carers of those loved ones, the comfort of hearing that level of compassion is central to the experiences of bereavement and to dealing with the associated grief. On a personal level, if I had not been able to be with Jay in his final hours then knowing that someone cared would have made it more comforting, so to all those nurses, doctors, care workers and professionals who took the time to be that hand of compassion, I and the rest of the world, we thank you, you are truly awe-inspiring.

Chapter 24

Cancer can follow a reasonably conventional pathway or it can be unpredictable and whilst the health professionals have a breadth of clinical expertise, they cannot foretell the future. There are clinical signs with regards to the process at the end of life but prior to this, it is difficult to know exactly.

With Jay, I had sixteen days following the terminal diagnosis to him passing away, this feels very unfair but looking back I would never have wished for him to suffer unnecessarily and when he died it was the right time as his quality of life was just not there anymore. You desperately don't want to say goodbye but at the same time, you question if it's fair for them to live, it is heart-breaking.

You feel every emotion you could imagine in those early days, you often feel numb and find it hard to articulate a specific emotion, so one minute you are sad and the next you are feeling a little more stoic and more resilient. I felt confused in those first few days, I understood what had happened and I was aware of what I needed to do but it was like an out of body experience, I was never quite sure how to 'feel'. What I can say is that it hurts and not just emotionally, it hurts physically too. It is a heavy and commanding feeling which is all-consuming, it feels like you have weights attached to you and that they are pulling you downwards. The skin on your body can feel itchy and almost like it's burning; it's a very weird and surreal experience and one which I can still feel to this day if I take myself back to that moment. You know you are breathing but every breath can feel laboured and like you need to take a big intake of air to try to compensate for feeling so out of control.

Grief is complicated, it needs to happen irrespective of what a person feels or thinks but it follows no set pathway, even when facing those hard emotions seems impossible it is part of the healing process but it never feels like that in the beginning.

One memory I have of those first few hours after Jay had been taken to his place of rest is of sitting in the armchair in my front room, I had asked for the hospital bed to be dismantled and put away as I couldn't stand being in the room with an empty bed. It was past midnight and everyone had left, I was sat on my own, looking at the space where the bed had been and looking at pictures of Jay on my phone. My phone had been constantly lighting up with messages from family and friends but I chose to put them on silent as I didn't have the words to reply.

I wanted and needed to cry but the tears were dry, my mind was frozen and my body could not move; the shock had set in. For a whole hour I sat in complete silence until it happened, one tear, then another and then I just cried until my whole body was tired. I somehow made it into bed that night, exhausted and overwhelmed. I fell asleep but awoke in the night with the realisation, "I am now a widow, what now?"

Chapter 25

Thanks to the endless conversations in the days before he could no longer communicate, I knew what to do for Jay's funeral and I was driven by his own words to ensure that I did everything I could to give him the best send-off I possibly could, I appreciate now how precious that time was. I had the gift of knowledge and I knew that everything I did was what he wanted which was invaluable.

Every day I prayed that he could come back to me but I was not in denial, I knew he had gone so I knew this was my opportunity to honour him by doing things exactly how he wanted. In the two weeks leading up to his funeral, I never stopped, I lived on a mixture of Adrenalin and sheer determination and strength to get me through each day but I needed to keep busy.

The day after he died, I had to make the short but painful visit to the funeral directors and whilst I knew what I needed to do logically, actually doing it was far harder than I could have imagined. As I sat in the funeral directors, I was shown an array of brochures and provided with information about all the different funeral options and although they were lovely, it was too overwhelming and all of sudden my mind went blank and making choices seemed impossible.

The focus I maintained for the funeral was that it wasn't my funeral, it was Jay's. He told me that he didn't want it too sad, instead, he wanted it to reflect his personality and the things he loved.

Jay had previously told me that he did not want a religious funeral so instead of hymns, I chose to show special photos of Jay alongside a very special song which meant a lot to both of us, Tom Walkers, *Just You and I*. His entrance was set to the *Top Gun* theme tune (Our favourite film) which was also the song we walked down the aisle to after getting married. When leaving the service, he was led out to the *Red Dwarf* TV theme tune and the *Tour of Duty* TV Theme tune *Paint it Black*, his two favourite TV shows.

On the day of the funeral, I woke up feeling surreal, I knew what I had to do but I didn't want to do it, it was the day to say goodbye, but I wasn't ready. I sat on my bed that day and I sprayed my bag with his body spray, I sat and took in the sweet aroma of the scent and let it take me back to the days where he would wear it, it was always my favourite. As I sat on the bed, I suddenly felt warm; it was a warm day but it wasn't that type of warmth, it was an inner feeling that to this day I can't describe apart from it being a spiritual feeling. I don't know what it was but it helped me get up, walk out the door and towards the cars which were now waiting outside. As we drove to the crematorium it was a quiet drive, it was simply sad. As we drove up the long driveway my eyes were drawn to all of Jay's friends standing outside the doors, they had matching football shirts on and were standing in line ready to bear the coffin. It was that sight which made the tears flow, it was seeing their sadness which made the reality way too real.

Jay was blessed with so many good friends and he had told me that his funeral was to be one of laughter and about all of his many holidays and nights out with the lads and that's exactly what we did. It was a mixture of laughter and the obvious sadness but it was everything he would have wanted and more. Jay loved his family but his friends were also important to him and he wanted his funeral to reflect this by focusing on the many good times, including some unheard stories of drunken antics that not even I had ever been told. The eulogies from his friends made everyone laugh and it was lovely to hear about how fun his life had been.

It still makes me smile that on his list of things to be buried with was his Manchester United Kit and his personally signed photo and message from the Manchester United manager, Sir Alex Ferguson. Oddly, he also wanted his Star Wars Luke Skywalker figure too. Personal letters were placed in his coffin from those that wanted to write them. I found writing mine comforting as I was able to say goodbye in my own words and it would forever be between just Jay and myself, this aided my grief as it allowed me to be honest about how I was feeling.

I am proud that I maintained all his wishes for his funeral and knowing that I did what he wanted gives me a great sense of inner peace. That's not to say that everyone agreed but I was driven by Jay's wishes so I never took those comments to heart, I knew that he would have been proud of me for upholding his wishes and for everyone who played a role in making it so unique.

It's hard to really put into words how you feel when you say goodbye to a loved one but it's a deep pain right in your heart, it feels so heavy and at times you think you will never breathe properly again but at the same time, you have a determination to get through it and somehow you do. Taking the time to make sure you do everything you need to do is important, those little memories really matter. My special memory was placing one of my silk roses from our wedding bouquet on his grave; to anyone else, it looks like a standard silk rose but to me, I know it symbols a love that will never leave me and I know that Jay would say the same if he was here.

As his coffin was lowered into the ground, my legs felt like they had no strength and I saw life as I knew it being lowered 6ft in the ground. I had no way of even contemplating how to move forward at that point. I do however remember my friend taking my hand afterwards and leading me to the waiting cars, I needed her to take control and I was so grateful for her support.

The wake was 'very Jay', there was food, music and lots of beer! I chatted to all the friends and family who had kindly joined us and smiled at hearing all of the stories' people were telling. Sadly, though my dear friends did keep offering me drinks which was never going to end well and, in the end, I admitted defeat and asked to go home. It was exactly how Jay would have wanted it, me being made to drink Vodka and his friends raising a glass of Jack Daniels. He definitely would have been smiling down on us all.

Chapter 26

I decided to go back to work very early, in fact, two days after the funeral, a lot of people said it was too early but I couldn't just sit at home thinking about what had happened, I needed to keep busy and for me that was work. It was hard I won't lie, I often found myself day-dreaming and having 'little moments' but it was good for me to have something to think about other than the fact I had just lost my husband. I was lucky to work with some truly wonderful colleagues who had also become my friends, their support is undeniably what got me through those long days; it's amazing what a cup of tea and a lot of cake can do to help normalise things a little.

In those early days, the evenings were the worst time, in the day I would be able to keep myself busy but, in the evenings, it was just so quiet. I would watch TV but at the end of the night, I wouldn't be able to tell you what I watched or what happened, I think it was just noise to keep me diverted from my own thoughts.

A difficulty that I experienced occurred in the days following Jay's death related to feelings of loneliness and abandonment. Up to and including the day of his funeral my entire focus had been solely on him, every second of my day was determined by his care needs and what I needed to do to enable him to feel more comfortable. Days were occupied by talking to Nurse's and specialists about his care and his wishes.

It's a very strange feeling as during that time, you are so tired both physically and mentally and part of you just wants to give up yet take that away and you almost crave for it to be back again.

Despite knowing he was going to die and being there when he did take his last breath, after I remember the eerie silence in the house and feeling truly alone for the first time in months, it was both surreal and completely disorientating. Up to that point no one had talked to me about 'me' and what support I could receive in those hours and days after my loss. This experience struck me in relation to how easy it could have been to become quite isolated and all consumed with my grief. I missed caring for him and being there when he needed me, all of a sudden life had stopped and strangely I didn't like it, at all.

My experience is unique to me however its prevalence is surprising, many people experience feelings of abandonment, loneliness and isolation after a bereavement and as such I feel it is important for professionals and communities to acknowledge the demand for good support for carers both during and after bereavement. Knowing a loved one is dying can be hard and understandably the focus is on the person who is dying but carers need care too.

When talking about bereavement it is important to be aware that it doesn't necessarily start at the point of death. *Anticipated grief* occurs when someone starts to process the facts and emotions in relation to knowing that someone is going to die prior to their death, it's a like a psychological warning to the brain to expect a traumatic experience so in readiness a person starts to process the fact that it will happen at some point.

Although this in some cases can help with the resulting bereavement the intensity of grief is essentially the same and the shock and denial associated with grief are still emotionally consuming.

Believe it or not, I consider myself very lucky, although caring for Jay over those thirteen months was hard and despite losing him, I was lucky as I had the time to prepare and, in a way, say goodbye. There are plenty of people out there who don't get the opportunity to say goodbye and I cannot begin to appreciate how that feels. Losing someone you love is one of the hardest events any person will ever go through but not having that opportunity to prepare, I imagine is very hard to understand.

Sudden or traumatic grief is difficult to process as there is no emotional preparation. I remember speaking to an old friend who lost her husband to suicide, whilst I was understandably empathic, I found myself not knowing what to say at first as my grief felt different to hers. We had both lost our husbands but the circumstances were so different but in reality, our grief was actually the same.

Grief is unique to each and every one of us, how we feel, how we act and how we process grief is something which cannot be definitively described, but what is the same for most people is that grief is hard and in the case of losing a close loved-one, it is life-changing.

Life is so precious and I know it sounds cliché but it really is, we really shouldn't take it for granted. We definitely can't wrap ourselves up in cotton wool or stop bad things from happening but just every now and then take a breath and look around and be grateful for just one thing per day, no matter how small it is. It could be the fact that you made yourself a hot drink and managed to drink it while it was still hot or that you took some time out to have a hot bath or read a book. Whatever you do, that one thing per day gives meaning and when you start to introduce meaning to your life again, then that's the start of the road to recovery.

Chapter 27

There are many websites and books that detail the grieving process, they offer a really good insight into what to expect and what is typical to experience. Whilst those books are incredibly helpful and informative, there is one thing they don't take into account and that's the unique nature of every one of us. Grief is not a solid process, it's different for every single person and whilst there are some common stages every person goes through, the length and intensity are unique.

For me, I chose to embrace being busy, I threw myself into organising the funeral, all the house paperwork, finance etc. As a person, I know I am quite stoic and resilient and although I was often told that it was okay to show a vulnerable side, I genuinely did want to just keep going and be strong, that was just my way of dealing with everything at the time.

In those early days, the saying which always made me smile was when people would say the quote 'get back to normal' but what is normal and how do you define it from person to person? The answer is, that you can't define it as normal has no one definition. I would love my life to be 'normal' but the truth is I don't actually know what it looks like and if anyone thinks they can specifically define it, then I would love to know the answer.

After losing someone you love, there are no right or wrong ways to approach how you see the future, you simply adapt in your own unique way. For me, I had to simply keep busy, so I returned to work and tried to maintain a routine to give me a structure to each day. Finding routine to the day offered a sense of purpose, but it didn't take away the pain, nor did it stop me from remembering.

I always felt desperately sad and although I kept busy, it didn't stop the heartache. I knew that no matter how many tears I cried, I couldn't bring him back, but I yearned for my old life back, I wanted to be caring for him again and to feel exhausted and stressed but at the same time, I knew that he was no longer suffering and that his passing meant he was no longer in pain and he was at rest.

Often the reality of losing someone is overwhelming, you understand the physical side of them not being there in the room with you but what I found the hardest was the emotional companionship. I was so used to having someone to talk to after a long day at work and having someone to turn to when I needed a friend that not having that was really difficult to overcome. Over time I found ways to ignore the silence but still to this day I always prefer to have music playing in the background, it's a way of the house not being silent.

Another stage I went through after the funeral was feeling angry. Anger is a phase which many people experience during bereavement, however the nature of the anger is what makes each person's experience unique. Anger can be directed in many different directions; you could be angry with a loved one for dying and leaving you alone or it could be that the death was within potential preventable circumstances and that you feel you or the loved one could have done more to prevent their death. The feelings of anger can be all-consuming; however, it is part of the grieving process and it is important not to rush through this stage as to be able to work through grief it is important to acknowledge and deal with the thoughts and emotions in order to move forward. Although often quite distressing and emotionally demanding anger is often a sign of resilience as a person is actively trying to come to terms with their loss.

My anger was directed at people telling me and assuming how I felt. Even though I know now that people were just trying to help me, I remember feeling incredibly angry that I was being told how I should act and that some of my decisions were not what others wanted or thought were right. That anger has now dissipated but at the time it was incredibly hard to get through.

Over the following two months, I started to adapt to life without Jay and overall, I was coping quite well, it was hard and it was strange but I know I had promised Jay that I would be okay. I always kept in mind the motto I had previously noted, "I will break, and I will fall but I will get up and in time I will walk forward again."

I was only 41 years old, so in lifetime terms, I was still young, I owed it to Jay to live my life and I had previously promised him that I would survive and I would be happy, I just wasn't sure at that precise moment how to be happy and how to forge a new life for myself and my boys but I knew in time it would happen at some point.

Chapter 28

During Jay's illness, I had been overwhelmed by the care provided by the palliative team from the local hospice, every day they came in to care for Jay and every single aspect of his care was assessed, monitored and constantly reviewed. The knowledge and their compassion was outstanding, they treated Jay like he was their only patient.

I was inspired by their attention to detail and their empathy towards both Jay and myself, and it was that which encouraged me to make some life-changing decisions in relation to my future.

Three months after the funeral, I took a massive leap of faith. My job had always been part of my identity and a massive part of my life but I knew I had to make a change.

I put in my notice at work and I signed up for a BSC (hons) Degree in Psychology with Counselling and other Counselling skills courses. It was a bold new start and it wasn't taken lightly; I had to take into account the financial impact as well as the personal sacrifices I would have to make, but I never regretted taking that massive leap, in fact it was the making of me.

Leaving work was incredibly hard; my work colleagues had been a pillar of strength to me and I was so grateful of their love and support. When I left, I remember crying more that night than I had done for the previous couple of months, I had gained some lifelong friends and to this day, I continue to be so very grateful for their support. I was incredibly proud to have been part of the Sustain team that made such a difference to the young people and families they supported. Working in the NHS and having that experience will stay with me forever, I was proud and still am proud to say I worked in such a wonderful service.

When I made the decision to start studying again and leave my job it was with the aim of completely changing my career. I decided that I wanted to use my experience to help others so I enquired about working in palliative care and bereavement support. I found that the nature of the study was motivating me and was so rewarding on a personal level. Even though I was learning about end-of-life care, it wasn't upsetting, it simply made me realise how important good quality palliative care was to those with life-limiting conditions. I realised that to be able to support people at such a difficult time was a privilege and that I had something in me that could not be read in a book or taught on a course, I had actual real-life and lived experience.

When a loved one passes away, you feel a real physiological pain and it is not like any pain you will ever experience, it's not helped by painkillers or kind words, it's a real, very physical pain and the only medicine is unfortunately time. Having experienced that pain for myself, I cannot begin to really explain it but I just know that when someone says to me that they feel like that they won't need to further explain it, I will be able to recognise those feelings. I cannot say that I will know exactly how they are feeling as this is unique to each person but I can definitely relate to it.

So, there I was, I was 42 years old, a widow and now technically unemployed or 'full-time mature student' as I called myself (it sounded better). But, for the first time in a long time, I was free and I felt happy and although not working was scary, there wasn't a doubt in my mind about my choices. Such a life-changing decision is not easy and I know I was very lucky to be in a position to be able to make those choices but that doesn't stop anyone from pursuing a dream or choosing to make a change to their life. It doesn't have to be a big leap of faith like mine; even one small change can have a huge effect on emotional and physical wellbeing.

Up to that month, I had found my own way of dealing with my grief but I had reached a point where I needed to step away from my grief and really focus on what was right for me and my future. The grief never left me and never will, I just made the decision to work alongside it rather than it dominating my life.

Chapter 29

Bereavement and grief are incredibly strong emotions and can be all-consuming, it touches every aspect of your life and there is no easy way to approach it. As human beings, we are all different, we all approach it in our own unique way and no way is wrong.

In the weeks and months which follow a bereavement, you have so many inevitable ups and downs; it is a tsunami of emotions at times. Songs on the radio, adverts on the TV, seeing friends in town and then the most emotional events...the firsts. Birthdays, Christmas, Anniversary's and all the other special days, they all have a significant impact on you.

In my first year after losing Jay, I had four firsts' in just two weeks. I had his birthday, Christmas, our wedding anniversary and New Year. To say I was dreading it was quite simply an understatement but it was genuinely alright and I somehow got through it. I made sure I was kept busy but at the same time, I did take some time out to reflect and think of him, we visited the graveside and we laid flowers and balloons and I said a prayer of thanks for him. It was hard and it was emotional but I knew that the only way to get through those special days was to be strong and to allow his precious memory to be remembered in a positive way.

During that time, I received so many beautiful messages from my friends and family and my tenacity, strength and my ability to work with the grief rather than let it be all-consuming was applauded by those around me. To this day, although I know that every single message was a blessing, it was hard to hear as I was just coping in the only way I knew how, I did not feel worthy of being told I was 'doing great'.

On the outside, I was indeed coping quite well but inside, I still missed Jay every minute of every day. I was still a whole spectrum of emotions but what I did learn (eventually) is t hat you should not be afraid to acknowledge those feelings.

It is healthy to be any one of the feelings associated with grief, be angry, be upset, be scared, maybe even feel lost in the new world you find yourself in but most of all don't ignore them, they are part of the recovery and part of the healing process, you need those emotions to make sense of the journey and to find a sense of meaningfulness again.

The hardest emotions to overcome are the feelings of being happy again, of smiling, of laughter and not feeling guilty about having a good day. These are the strongest emotional feelings as these come with a whole bucket load of guilt. The guilt that you can't be happy because you are in mourning, that you need to spend an expected amount of time grieving and that smiling is frowned upon because you should be sad. You start to ask yourself questions like 'when it is acceptable to do normal things like going out with friends' etc and if someone sees me smiling or laughing will they think bad of me and think I don't care. These questions sound bizarre maybe but trust me they are the real questions that you ask yourself on a daily basis.

For a couple of months, I sat at home thinking how do I move on, how do I begin to comprehend a life without my best friend and the man with who I wanted to spend the rest of my life. I don't think there was a defining moment but I just know that one day I decided that I needed to remember what Jay had told me over the last year. He told me I had to pick myself up and to be who I wanted to be both personally and in my career. He told me that he knew I would always love him but I needed to be happy and if I met someone else in the future, I needed to try to be happy. Now saying this and doing it are completely different but I will never forget those conversations.

One of the things that struck me was that no one really mentions that throughout the grief and bereavement journey, one minute you can be just fine and then all of a sudden there is an explosion of emotion over something so small. At first, it's quite scary and you are convinced that it's a massive setback but I have started to understand that it is just part of the journey and I have to accept that there will be days when I feel down and upset but then on the other side, I will have days when I feel great and really positive.

Chapter 30

Hitting six months post bereavement was a strange milestone, whilst six months isn't really a long time, I was adapting to my new life and I was doing alright, I was immersed in my studies and enjoying a few too many coffee and cake mornings with my friends. I still thought and missed Jay every single day but I always will, and that's something that cannot be lost or forgotten. I regularly had periods when I would get upset and the way I got through those times is to acknowledge them.

Rather than ignoring my thoughts, I learnt to accept them and if I found myself becoming upset, I would take time out to sit and recognise those feelings. If I needed to cry, I cried, I would look at photos and remember our happy memories but also, I took time to remember the harder times.

Life was very different but having a focus was incredibly important and for me, at the time it was my study, it was and still is my escape and although stressful when it's deadline week, it has been extremely fulfilling. It offered and still offers me a sense of purpose and a way forward.

I am so very grateful to Jay as he has gifted me this opportunity to change my career and to go back to university, he gave me the strength to make this massive leap of faith and to take a chance on life, every day I remind myself that my life now is possible because of him.

As a person Jay was incredibly selfless; he would always put others first. His kindness showed no limits and everyone who knew him knew that if they needed a friend or some advice, Jay was your go-to man. I remember just four months after meeting him I needed surgery on my knee and despite us being in the 'honeymoon phase' of our relationship, he cared for me like we had been together for years. Unfortunately, that was tested more than a few times over the years due to multiple ankle operations but never once did he moan; he simply cared for me and showed me the most wonderful compassion when I was in pain or needed him, he really was amazing.

When people ask me now what Jay was like, it's very hard not to smile and just think lovely thoughts, it used to upset me but now I simply love the fact that I can talk so positively about him and shout to the world about how wonderful he was. It's very hard when someone you love dies, to even contemplate smiling and to talk about them in such a positive way. When they are ill or after they have died the emotions are so raw, the future feels almost bleak and you do question the reasons you have to carry on. At that time, it's not about ignoring those feelings, you have to go through that and unfortunately, you have to experience that awful feeling of loss and pain which at times is truly unbearable. It's very hard to even try to put those feelings into words, many books and articles definitely try and they do capture the essence of grief but the reality is so different.

The reality is, grief is unique, it is not one set of rules and certainly has no time limit, don't beat yourself up because another person was okay after a couple of months, everyone is different. Bereavement is a process and within reason, there are steps that everyone goes through but they are the black and white of the process, the grey bits in-between is what we as human beings have to experience in our own way.

What I did learn is that sometimes it's good to acknowledge your inner strength, I have certainly always been quite a stoic person but there are times when even the strongest and most resilient of people need to ask for help. Rather than a sign of weakness, asking for help is actually the sign of enormous strength. It takes courage to ask for help and at six months, I did just that.

Chapter 31

It's very hard to really know how to look into the future and see that everything is going to be alright, you know it's possible but sometimes something just stops you and it's hard to get past those barriers at times. It was around this time that I was very lucky to be offered the chance of some counselling. I willingly requested the counselling thinking it would be helpful and that it would be good to talk to someone neutral who didn't know me and had no preconceived ideology of both myself and my situation.

Meeting the counsellor for the first time, I couldn't fully relax and although I was listening to her, I couldn't get past my own emotional barriers, which was frustrating at times, then after a couple of sessions, I started to listen more intently as some of what she was saying was making sense to me. By session four, the penny had dropped and I realised that to truly move on I had to confront some pretty deep fears and experiences from my past. By acknowledging my insecurities, I could give my future my full focus.

In that fourth session, she gave me a really good analogy which I still use to this day.

Imagine your grief is like a really bad cut on your hand, its bleeding, it's sore and it won't heal, so you put a plaster over it. The trouble is, when we put that plaster on, it hides the sore and painful cut (The grief), it shields us and for a time because that plaster is covering the wound, we can pretty much carry on as normal and pretend everything is okay. But, the truth is that as long as that plaster is on the wound, it cannot heal, it has no chance to breathe and to start the recovery process.

On that day, it was like a 'light bulb' moment for me; I had without a doubt 'put a plaster on my life and my grief' and I was refusing to even begin to take it off.

At the next session, we started to talk about how it would feel about airing that wound and starting to peel off the plaster. Taking that plaster off would be painful and I knew I would resist it but deep down I knew she was right, I had to deal with this as if I didn't, I would never fully move on.

From that moment on that process began and little by little that plaster slowly started to come off and as it was slowly removed, the wound (Grief) started to heal. It was by no means easy and even with my tenacity, I did and still do fight it, after all, who wants to willingly let someone open a wound that is covered and not causing any problems.

My debate with the counsellor at that point was complex; I did genuinely want to rip the plaster off but at the same time, I needed to do it in my own time and come to terms with everything in my own way. The myriad of emotions at that point was overwhelming and trying to understand my thoughts about everything was confusing.

Sitting with a counsellor week by week you do start to process things differently and you start to make more sense about all of those conflicting thoughts and feelings. Whilst it's a good feeling to understand more clearly, it's often met with a sense of bewilderment too as it's all so new and it's hard to process how it will all work out in the long term.

It was halfway through my sessions that I truly grasped that my grief had not just appeared seven months ago when Jay passed away and it wasn't just when we had the terminal diagnosis, it had been with me the full 18 months of his illness.

Before Jay passed away, I had a level of anticipated grief in that I knew he was dying and therefore was subconsciously preparing for his passing, even though on a conscious level, I still had hope and wished that a miracle would happen. I realise now that my grief had been with me for a long time. When I sat down and thought about what my counsellor was saying about me coping really well, I understood that I was coping well because I had been unconsciously prepared long before his actual passing.

Bereavement and grief are not quick processes and there are days when you feel okay and you cope really well but there are also days when the feelings become overwhelming and all-consuming. It's only when you come to terms with the fact that it's not a straightforward path that you can start to come to terms with everything.

There is no magic wand and there is no set process, which for someone like me is frustrating and annoying as I need to have that control within my life. Grief can take control away and that is really hard to come to terms with. Time, as they say, is the healer but anyone who likes answers knows that time is also the hardest answer to hear and accept.

Chapter 32

One of the feelings no one really talks about when you are on this journey is that you also become slightly more paranoid about your own health. Even though you know you are physically fine, health anxiety is a very real and unforgiving repercussion of the experience.

What seemed like a normal day, one Sunday turned out to be a curveball I didn't expected. After having a bit of a girly afternoon, I decided to paint my toenails but to do that I needed to remove the varnish already on. That very simple and innocent act changed my day. Underneath my varnish, I noticed a small black spot on my nail. At first, I thought it was just a mark but I soon realised it was quite a large round black mark on my toenail.

The consequence of having lived with someone with cancer is that all of a sudden everything has the potential to be cancer when you are ill yourself, whether you like it or not. Of course, like most people, I did look on the internet to check to see if resembled anything potentially suspicious and there, sure enough, were pictures that looked exactly like my toe.

The next day I called my GP to get an appointment, logically knowing that it was probably nothing but still worrying that it was something potentially harmful. Sitting in the waiting room at the surgery took me back to so many painful memories, all of a sudden, I was in that chair and I was the one who could have cancer, it was truly the most frightening experience.

As I walked in, my heart was beating and I was physically shaking. After an examination of the said toe, the doctor confirmed that thankfully although he agreed it did look suspicious visually, he was confident it wasn't cancer. I did, however, need to measure it for a month to make sure it didn't grow or change in colour or texture. That month I think I looked at that toe more times than I can even begin to count but over time it did thankfully fade and disappear.

What made that month so hard was that I didn't tell a single person of my discovery, and I dealt with it alone, something I now realise was wrong as I had people around me who would have supported me. At the time I automatically went into my own world, something which is common with people who have experienced bereavement due to a health condition. The experience changes you, even if you don't realise it.

Chapter 33

I wish I knew what caused 'bad days'; those days where small problems are huge and minor irritations seem to feel like horrendous mountains to climb. One day on a cold frosty morning in February, it was just one of those days; the dogs would not settle and kept barking at every little noise and I was trying to study but I might as well have been studying it in a foreign language as my brain refused to understand the logic behind the words. It was winding me up and was causing a really unhealthy level of anxiety which was unsettling and quickly became all-consuming.

The answer that day was to close the study books, order some food in and pour a glass of wine and admit that rather than fighting, I just go with it. Although I have to admit one drink would have sufficed, it was definitely a more than one glass kind of day.

Bad days will always happen and despite our great efforts to try to overcome them, sometimes you just have to admit defeat and say, tomorrow is another day. Unfortunately, there were quite a few of those days at first but they have happily become less frequent as time passed.

That week, I saw the counsellor again and the words just flowed in respect of my awful week. She did, however, come up with another good analogy which once again I found really useful. She reminded me that bad days are just a prelude to a good day and that my track record of getting through bad days was always 100% and that I should never forget that.

Positive thinking is great but let's face it, it's hard work sometimes and there were definitely times when I just felt like telling people to shut up and go away.

On those bad days, everything was an uphill struggle, every song on the radio reminded me of Jay and every person I saw in town was holding hands and looking blissfully happy. I was constantly reminded that I had no one there to just give me a hug and say 'Jo, you're okay'. Jay used to give brilliant hugs like that, he would just hold me incredibly tight and often not say a word but I knew he just got me and that he knew I just needed him to make all the bad go away; I still miss that more than I could even begin to put into words.

Loneliness is one of the major feelings in bereavement and grief, for some it can be all-consuming and when I hear stories of people who have felt uncontrollable sadness, I do understand that completely.

I was reading a story recently of an elderly couple; they had been together for just over seventy years and in all that time apart from the war, they had never spent a single night away from each other. They had a wonderful extended family with three children and multiple grandchildren and great-grandchildren, they had their health issues but for their age, they were in relatively good health. One day, without warning, their lives changed forever. The husband suffered a stroke and passed away and all of a sudden, a once blissfully happy ninety-year-old was thrown into a life she couldn't imagine. What followed was both incredibly sad but so heart-warming. Just twelve hours after losing her husband, she too passed away. The cause of death was a heart attack but most clinicians would call it by its non-medical name which is simply a 'Broken Heart'. Later that month, they were buried together, forever to be as one.

Whilst this story is so sad, it just makes you realise how strong we have to be after losing a loved one, our hearts are broken and that invisible pain is at times unbearable but we can survive and we can carry on, it just takes time. The heart will have a scar permanently but it will keep beating and it will learn to maybe even love again.

One day I know my children and maybe even grandchildren will read this story and whilst I am sure they will be moved by the sadness I have experienced; I hope that they will see how strong we can all be in the face of adversity. Life isn't perfect but then again, it's not bad either, yes, we will have great sadness in our lives and yes at times we will feel as if our hearts are broken and we cannot mend or move on but life is precious and it is a gift which we should not take for granted. The greatest lesson we will ever learn in life is to simply live and love life.

Metaphorically, you could think of life like a garden, we have an idea of how we want it to look like and we can be meticulous in our planning and our actions, however, life has a tendency to grow a few weeds sporadically which at times can be a little out of control. The garden can sometimes not look its best but there are also times when that garden blooms. In essence, our 'garden/life' is colourful and beautiful and life can be incredibly good but like a garden, there are times when life doesn't always turn out as we planned but if we take the time to nurture it and be patient, then quite often things turn out okay in the end.

When I talk to people, I often say how lucky I am and people look at me strangely, they cannot comprehend how I can be lucky given what I have lost, but in reality, I choose to look at what I have gained and what I have to look forward too. I wish I could say that it was easy but it's not, but in time, it is possible.

By looking forward, it gives me hope that I can be me again and that although I now have a scar on my heart, life will be okay.

I can understand how some people will say that my positive attitude is amazing but then there are also some people who will think I'm talking a load of rubbish and that it's impossible to get over something so big so fast. Truth is no one is wrong as there is no right way or wrong way to deal with death; it's unique to each and every one of us. I'm just dealing with it in my own way and in my time, just like every single other person in a situation like mine.

When you sit and think about grief, it's very hard to appreciate the enormity of it. My counsellor recommended to me that I take dedicated time each day or week to think about Jay and/or about my grief journey. Whilst at first, I struggled with that concept I am slowly learning to appreciate why it is so important. Life carries on whether we like it or not, the house still needs cleaning, the dogs still need walking and the food shopping still needs to be done. We can choose to ignore all those things for a while and that's okay at first but eventually, we do need to create a 'new normal'. When you do, at first, it's incredibly hard work, it's an emotional and physical effort to even start those jobs but it really does get easier with time, however does it completely go away? No.

When faced with such a life-changing event, I often wonder how on earth I survived and how I remain so positive. I would love to provide the answer but actually, I have no idea, it just happened, I found a way to adapt and to live life as best I could. There is no answer and there is no prescription for the remedy, unfortunately like I keep saying, it is that very annoying word (which everyone hates), 'Time'.

In summary, think of life as a fairground roller-coaster ride, sometimes it's exciting and you look forward with a smile on your face and a positive anticipation of the future but sometimes that positivity turns to fear and the only thing you can do is just hold on, shut your eyes and know that the scary times won't last.

Chapter 34

As the months go by, you start to slowly think about the future and how it may look for you moving forward. Even getting to that point seems unthinkable in the beginning but when you do it feels quite overwhelming knowing that you now have a whole new range of decisions and emotions to face.

I remember sitting on the sofa one day and I was casually watching tv when a programme came on about dating, I watched with amusement, smiling at the couples on their first dates and their awkwardness. I didn't really think about anything while I was watching it but that night, I lay in bed thinking that maybe one day that might be me, it was scary, very scary!

The thought of meeting someone else is indeed very scary and for those who have lost a loved one, it's most definitely the question that has no right answer. At the end of the day, we did not choose to lose the person we love, we didn't stop loving them when they died, we still love them now and that will never change. I questioned how on earth it would be possible to love someone as much as Jay and how I could even contemplate feeling like that ever again.

The answer is still one which still makes me think but I'm not scared of it anymore, I feel that I do deserve to be happy and that I do deserve to feel love again.

I will never be able to get over losing Jay and he will always be my soulmate but the awful truth is that I am still here and I need to find a way to live my life as best as possible and that includes being happy again. If it takes six months or six years, time should not be prescriptive as let's face it, life doesn't exactly come with a rule book; we get up each day and we have no idea what the day holds, that's life.

After watching the programme on TV finding love again was on my mind but I wasn't at all sure how I would feel and if I would compare them to Jay all the time. To test myself, I joined a dating site online; it was the first time I'd ever even tried one so I had no idea what to expect. I had no intention really of meeting anyone but I guess I was curious about it all.

In the first few weeks, I found it very confusing, I looked at all these different 'men' who were supposedly compatible with me but no one looked remotely nice. When I looked at a photo or read their description, I instantly compared them to Jay as in my eyes he was the benchmark (Which was incredibly high). It was a mixture of emotions, some days it was just funny and I did chuckle to myself over some of the messages I received and other days, it would make me sad and at times quite upset.

Setting up a profile is a strange thing, what you put is the usual; love walking, good sense of humour, love cooking and going the movies etc. What you actually need to write is 'Lonely widow seeks a partner who will be no one like the

147

person they want to be with, seeks good company and someone with likes everything that my soulmate loved. Must know me inside out and be able to just know when you need a hug' – that could really go on and on.

A couple of months in, I decided to test the water and go on a date. I remember feeling so nervous and trying to find something to wear which was deemed appropriate, was frankly just stressful. Considering I hadn't been on a date in thirteen years, it went okay but I was left feeling confused about whether it was the right thing or not to do. I was quite disheartened thinking that dating was just going to mess with my head even more and that what I didn't need right now was more complications and stress in my life but nevertheless, at least I had tried it.

A couple of weeks later, I decided that what I needed was a night out with my friend so that's exactly what I did. On the way into town, the taxi driver started the night on such a high by making me smile, "So, you're 'out-out' tonight then love." I hadn't heard that expression in ages and I just replied 'yes' with a huge grin on my face.

For the first time in ages, I actually felt confident about being me; I had the classic little black dress on, beautiful yellow heels and the brightest lippy I could find. We had such a good night, I laughed, I danced and after a few too many drinks, I did maybe even get a random midnight kiss from a rather good-looking guy we had been talking to…did I feel guilty…? Absolutely not, it was bloody great! I was me again and it felt amazing.

Chapter 35

So, as we all know life is unpredictable and out of the blue something happened which changed my outlook completely. Whilst I had been dipping my feet into the dating world, I was slowly thinking that maybe it wasn't for me and that I just wasn't ready. It had been 'interesting' shall we say, but something was missing.

I knew that comparing men to Jay would be wrong as frankly no one in the world would even begin to come close. I still looked at his photos admiring his lovely smile, his cheeky grin and his beautiful eyes; he really was just the most perfect man. I had no idea after going on a few dates that anyone could truly come close to that relationship.

Over time, I did start to accept that I wasn't replacing Jay but the future version of me could not physically stand by his side anymore, I had to learn to walk alone and maybe even towards someone else. It is only when I accepted that thought that I truly felt ready to properly try to move on. When that happens isn't a fixed timeframe, it just happens when it happens.

That testament became a little more realistic when I met a man for a date one night. We talked for hours and we clicked straight away and by the end of the night, we had agreed to a second date. For about six weeks, life wasn't about my grief, it was about hope and looking forward, it certainly boosted my confidence and we really enjoyed each other's company, he showed me that I could be happy and that it was possible to be me again, I was allowed to smile, laugh and feel loved.

Although that relationship didn't work out, I was lucky enough to gain a true friend who I still see to this day. He gave me the gift of confidence and for that I will always be grateful.

I have at times, struggled to come to terms with the fact I am ready to move on and the emotions of guilt have been overwhelming. I have also struggled to accept that not everyone will accept my choices and my decisions, there will always be people who judge me and think it's too soon. I have spent many nights lying in bed thinking about what people will say and how I will be perceived. My worst fear was that people would think that my love for Jay was not genuine, the thought of that kept me awake for many nights. Truth is that the people who know me would not doubt my love for Jay; they know my heart literally broke when he had his diagnosis and when he passed away, my life changed forever.

For those people who did judge me and did not understand, I question if they really know me and if they do truly love me (It took twelve sessions of counselling to instil that in me). I knew that there would be people who would not understand and those are the people who chose to walk away from me and distance themselves which I don't understand but I do accept.

Whilst I do understand how they feel, I also know that Jay wanted me to be happy and to live my life still and I should not feel guilty for doing just that. To those that chose to walk away and not accept my decisions, I feel no anger, I just feel sadness. I know exactly what Jay wanted for me and the boys, in fact, he made me agree to a set of wishes that I had to complete after he died. Some I could do straight away, some would take weeks, months and maybe even years but those promises will always stand and I am adamant that every single request will be fulfilled.

As a widow you do not stop loving the person you have lost, you still love them but you cannot be 'in love' with them as they are not with you, so to develop feelings for someone else you have to develop a way of still holding on to that love but developing a way of loving a new partner at the same time.

It's very hard to put into words how you begin to like/love again and the only analogy I can relate to is that of being a parent. When you have a child the love you feel is all-consuming. When you have another child, you simply can't imagine loving that child as much as the first but you do, you develop that same love for both children and that is the same for any further children.

I still think of Jay every single day, I still visit his graveside on poignant days and I still cry when I think about the loss I have experienced. Truth is that grief is multi-dimensional; it is different for every single one of us. There is no right way or wrong way to deal with the huge range of emotions it brings. I just know that despite everything to date I would not change a single second; it has made me who I am and I know that I can use that as a strength rather than a weakness.

Unfortunately, general societal expectations are such that as a widow it can be expected to be in mourning until some deem it is okay to move on. Dependent on the circumstances that could be a few weeks, a few months or even years (Cultural and spiritual beliefs may be relevant here so I can only speak from my experience rather than as the voice of the general population).

Truth is there are no real processes and no real guidelines as to what is 'normal' and what isn't. All I know is that I am still grieving Jay but I have learnt to accept the fact he died and that despite loving him still, my life has to move on regardless of any internal or external influences. I do, however, take something from the experience and that is that I developed a new stoicism for life, in that I did learn to listen and respect people's viewpoints, but at the end of the day, I had to put myself first for the first time in a long time, it has been hard and if I'm being honest, I'm still working on that bit.

I knew from day one that if I were to be in a relationship there would always be people who did not agree and that I would receive some differing opinions. I was ready for the negativity but what I wasn't ready for was how much it hurt me emotionally. When the negative comments came, and they did, it really hurt, more than I can ever put into words.

Whenever I received criticism, I always listened and tried to take on board their opinions as after all, everyone is allowed free speech. What was difficult is the aftermath of those comments, when I was able to sit and reflect on them. I do understand that most people thought that meeting someone new was too soon but that's just not how relationships work.

I really wanted to accept the comments and to be respectful but it's so hard when you are trying to be happy but everyone around you is throwing negativity at you, it is more challenging than people give it credit for.

Throughout that period, I held onto a few poignant facts which kept me strong. I had promised Jay that no matter what I would be happy and despite his passing, I would love again one day but more than that, I made a promise to myself that I would believe in myself and know that I am allowed to be happy.

On reflection of all the negativity though, I have also been supported by some absolutely wonderful friends and family who accept my decisions and have always stood by my choices, even if they thought they were a bit rash sometimes. There were specific groups of friends who from day one supported me and have never left my side, for that alone I have no words as without that moral support, I really don't think I could have got through all emotional ups and downs.

Chapter 36

Overall, my life is beyond rich, I have two talented and wonderful sons who I am incredibly proud of. I have a loving family who have stood by me and held me up when I needed that strength and I have my amazing friends who have seen me through the dark times but then held my hand while I took steps back into the light.

To anyone facing the same situation, it is hard to offer advice as there is actually no one answer as to how you rebuild and move on after losing someone special. I guess the truth is that you don't ever really move on, you just have to take a different pathway and see where you go. Sometimes that new pathway is so new that it's incredibly scary, sometimes it's full of the most wonderful surprises, you just don't know until you decide to walk forward and see where it takes you.

My life is just one of many; so many people in this world are going through what at the time feels like an inferno of uncertainty and sadness. Everyone is different and we all have our story to tell, this is simply mine. I know that honestly my next life story is only just beginning. Is it scary? Absolutely but is it worth the determination? Definitely!

I feel happiness and I feel contentment, which are two things I never thought would be possible after losing my amazing husband. When you experience any level of bereavement in the beginning, the rawness and pure pain are all-consuming, it hurts like the most unimaginable pain and it is hard to think of the next day never mind the future.

It is true, time is a healer, however, you cannot forget time nor can you erase it, it simply always exists but what time does provide is the space to explore your emotions and to start to understand how to live alongside them rather than behind them.

Life can be beautiful and it can also be very dark, I guess the secret is to learn to find the light in the darkness but at the same time, appreciating that life is like the sun and moon, there will always be darkness and there will also be light, it is an eternal circle of life and the two have to work together in order to create the day.

I will survive as I am stronger and I will carry on because I have resilience. No matter how you experience grief, allow it to happen and allow yourself to feel that pain because ultimately it does make you stronger and although never the same, life can be beautiful again.

Chapter 37

So, where does my story end? Truthfully, it's an ongoing process from which I am still learning and living with. My life up to now has certainly had its ups and downs, at times it's been like a rollercoaster with no off switch but as you will have read throughout my story, you will have realised that we are never in full control of our lives. Life evolves whether we like it or not. However, it is true what they say, when you are least expecting it, something wonderful can happen which will just change your world in ways which you previously thought impossible.

That change for me came from an unexpected but amazing new relationship which once again changed how I saw not only the world around me but how I saw myself.

One thing that changes when you are widowed is that even when you have gained some confidence, deep down you still question anyone ever loving you as much as the person you lost. You can portray a confident person but underneath the bravado you are still haunted by a sense of grief and reluctance to fully move on.

I realised straight away upon meeting Gareth that although I had been honest with myself previously maybe I had not taken the time to really genuinely accept the fact that someone could love me unconditionally.

I was always trying to make sense of what I wanted for my future but new relationships as a widow were just scary and confusing. When you speak to friends, family or colleagues you willingly listen and comfort them while they tell you about their awful divorce or how their relationship broke down and how it was really traumatising. Whilst those situations are no less upsetting, it is so different to someone actually dying. Cancer does not give a choice, especially when it's terminal. It doesn't give you the option to carry on or the chance to 'talk about it and make it work'. You just simply lose the love of your life with no choice in the matter, so when people talk to me about heartbreak, I do, of course, respect that it does hurt but the death of a loved one is indescribable, it's hard to find something to compare it to.

Meeting my partner was nerve racking but also exciting. We met at Chasewater which is a large expanse of water in Staffordshire, as I sat on the bank waiting for him to arrive, I was a bag of nerves, but I shouldn't have been nervous. After half an hour of walking we were chatting like we had known each other for months, not minutes, we hit it off instantly. It was the most magical day and one which is still very special to us both, however it didn't come completely pain-free! In my attempt to 'look good' I thought it would be a good idea to wear some beautiful white strappy high heel sandals to my date, they complemented my outfit perfectly and I felt great. The downside however is that walking around a 3-mile lake on gravel and grass is not conducive to wearing heels, so by half way round I was slightly regretting my choice of footwear. As we sat down on the grass in the beautiful sunshine on our return to the main entrance, I remember Gareth realising the mistake I had made so I relented and took the sandals off, much to my relief. The day went by in a flash and after four hours of chatting in the sunshine it was time to head of home. That day started the next chapter in my life.

In the months that followed I continued to grow in confidence, I was finding my way through my grief and it finally felt like I was moving forward and that I could allow myself to be happy and finally to be me.

I knew that Gareth loved me for who I am now, he respected my past and allowed me to talk about it and actively listened when I felt down or needed to talk.

He is not afraid to ask about Jay and will encourage me to talk about our life together whilst at the same time encouraging me to look to the future.

Talking is a way of acknowledging the past but living in the future and I cannot underestimate how important that is if you are in a new relationship. There are still times that I find it hard to talk about Jay but at the same time, I feel immensely proud to talk about him and to ensure that his legacy lives on through myself, Lewis and Oliver. I actually smile now when I talk about him, I enjoy re-living stories of his drunken antics with his friends and remembering the amazing holidays we had together.

My new relationship with Gareth is both loving and special and I cannot and will not compare it to the one I had with Jay, however, what I do know is that I have found happiness. My heart will forever be broken and the scar will always be there, it will never be the same again but I know that Gareth sees that scar and that he will forever respect that it is an important aspect of who I am now as a person. Jay is embellished in my very soul, he is woven into my heart indefinitely but I have to acknowledge that I have found love again and, in that love, my heart will beat stronger every day. I am being the person I should be and that's 'me', I embrace the fact that I can smile, I can laugh and I can feel love again.

I am simply happy and happiness is an incredibly valuable emotion and in I am so happy that I will get to share that happiness with my friends and family as in October 2021 he did in deed get down on one knee and propose! Knowing how much I love the sea, he officially proposed in Cornwall on the top of a cliff in Bude, it was so special and romantic and I couldn't have wished for anything more. In that moment I knew my life was going to be okay and that Jay would be so happy for me, he would be comforted that I have found love again but mostly that Gareth loves me for me, which is all he wanted for me.

In celebration of my new life and my continuing and multiple leaps of faith, (plus a little bit of rebelling in my aging years maybe!) I decided that a fitting tribute would be to show my journey in some new tattoos. I always loved tattoos but was never brave enough to actually sit in the artist's chair and have one done, so to celebrate my new beginning, I made the appointment, although that first appointment inadvertently turned into six over the following year.

My first tattoo was a tree of life to symbolise my past and future journey through life; it had a heart on the tree roots to symbolise Jay being part of my life, along with the names of my children. The second was a blowing dandelion with the French wording 'Avec Toi Je Suis Moi' which translates as 'With You, I Am Me'; a fitting tribute to Gareth for helping me find 'Jo' again.

The third and biggest tattoo is a rising Phoenix, I chose this to symbolise rising above adversity and my continued journey. The fourth was a simple but beautiful floral bracelet design on my wrist, I really wanted this one to have a special meaning like the others but the truth is, I just liked it and thought why not. Number five was the symbol unconditional love and the sixth was the Buddhist Unalome symbol along with a lotus flower signifying finding peace after life's twists and turns. Sorry Dad, but I have to admit I'm already looking at number seven.

The following months were a journey of finding myself again but this time it was in a relationship. My study was going incredibly well and I was passing all of my courses, often with distinctions, I felt like I was finally finding my future and for the first time in a long time I was smiling more than I was crying and I was dreaming about a future rather than living in the past.

Chapter 38

In the days of diagnosis, treatment and in palliative care, it is difficult to even begin to think about love and the future, it is incomprehensible to even consider having feelings for another partner but as I was proving it does happen. It takes time but when you reach that point where those feelings are real and you know that you can love again, the feeling of warmth and contentment is overwhelming.

Jay left this earth knowing that he wasn't ready, he had achieved so much in his life and he knew he still had so many more adventures to experience and to enjoy. Looking back now, I am able to appreciate the difference he made to the people he loved. Towards the end, we spoke at great length about what my future would look like and he was quite specific about the direction I needed to take. He also spoke to the boys to encourage them to follow their dreams and to always think big, the world was their oyster and they needed to always strive to be the best version of themselves that they could be. His legacy is one that fills me with immense gratitude; he instilled in me and the boys that our future would not be one of sadness but one of hope and optimism.

When I look back at our journey, it fills me with immense pride to see how far we have all come and how through the toughest of times we have continued to fulfil that legacy and make him proud.

In his honour, Lewis graduated with a first-class degree at University in Games Art. My youngest son is currently at university successfully studying a degree in professional Photography.

As for me, academically I have successfully gained multiple qualifications in Bereavement Counselling and Thanatology, palliative care and end-of-life care and I continue to pass all of my modules within my Psychology University Degree. I was delighted to be awarded my accreditation following my successful completion of my Level 4 Counselling Diploma and have also now completed the training to qualify as a Bereavement Volunteer with the national bereavement charity. I have also been lucky enough to have been accepted for a placement with a wonderful local bereavement and loss service which I am incredibly proud to be part of as they offer the most rewarding service to the local people of Stafford.

I started a job as a CareGiver in 2021 which has given me a sense of purpose again. Despite working in health and social care settings most of my working life I had never worked directly with clients so it was another leap of faith for me to do something completely different. My work has introduced me to some of the most truly wonderful people, I have realised that I have sense of humour which all my clients love and that simple acts of kindness go a long way in providing quality of life to someone who is maybe struggling with their health or wellbeing. Walking in to someone's home and seeing them smile when I just simply make a cup of tea and spend time talking to them isn't work, it's a privilege.

My journey has not been easy however being able to use my experience to help others has always been my dream. If I can help just a handful of people in their journey then my journey through all its ups and downs will be worth it.

So, on the whole my journey has been every emotion I could ever imagine but on a personal level, I am simply happy again, my life has meaning and it is full of love and true belonging. Meeting Gareth has given me a new lease of life and whilst I never forget my past, I am so excited to see what my future holds both in my relationship and my career.

Jay's legacy is that he may have left us in person but he gave us all a future, he allowed us all to appreciate that life is precious and that despite the bad days, life can be worthwhile. We have the gift of life and he wanted us to use that and to always be happy.

I for one would not change a single moment of my past; it has made me who I am today and even when I have made mistakes and maybe not got things right, I am grateful for every moment and every experience.

Someone asked me recently how I got over the grief of losing Jay, my answer surprised them. I am not over the grief at all, I am still living with it every day, it is just that I now use my grief to give myself a purposeful direction and to remind myself that in the darkest of days, I found a reason to carry on and with those reasons, I found meaning to my life again.

I cannot give you direct advice but what I can say is this, never give up hope, even when the clouds are dark and your heart is breaking. It takes time and there is no stop clock and there are certainly no rules about what is right or wrong. Take it hour by hour and day by day, acknowledge both the good days and the bad days and more importantly never give up hope.

Now, technically this was going to be the end of my story but life, as we know, is full of unexpected curve balls and surprises. Sixteen months after losing Jay, I was to find out myself just how real cancer is and how it feels to be on the other side of the caring relationship.

Chapter 39

Life was good, I was in a loving relationship and I was finally beginning to think that my life looking forward was one of happiness and hope and whilst I still visited Jay's graveside and still thought of him on a daily basis, I was able to focus on my life as it was and was really starting to smile again.

Whilst I had always had niggling health problems, I put them down to my age, I didn't worry and I certainly didn't visit the doctor, however, after four months of some niggling issues, I decided that maybe a trip to the doctors was needed.

A barrage of tests later, I found myself sitting in the surgery talking to my doctor. What followed had the potential to change all of my future plans in just one sentence. I sat listening to the doctor telling me how during my examination she had seen an abnormal area and that in her opinion and given my symptoms, she needed to advise that she did worry about it being cancerous and that she would refer me urgently to the hospital.

In that brief moment in time, I was thrown back to sitting in the Endoscopy suite with Jay, waiting to hear his diagnosis, all of those sickening, stomach-churning feelings were back but this time it was me, this time I could potentially say the words, "I have cancer." It felt surreal.

I felt numb, my heart was beating and I had no idea whether I needed to cry or fall to the ground. Walking out of the surgery, my mind was a sea of uncertainty, I tried to convince myself that I had not heard it right, maybe I was wrong but reality soon hit home when I walked out the surgery doors and realised that this was real, I was no longer the carer, I was the patient.

As I got in the car, my first thoughts turned to my boys, how on earth could I begin to tell them I was now potentially ill and then there was Gareth, how would I tell him he would potentially need to go through the same journey as I went through with Jay.

I wanted to desperately speak to Gareth but I knew he was at work and wouldn't be able to answer his phone so I rang my friend. I could hardly speak but through the deep breaths, I muttered the words, "They think it could be cancer, I'm so scared."

I had definitely rung the right friend as she instantly knew what to say, we talked about the possibility of it being cancer but also that I had to remember it might not be.

After speaking with her, I sat in the car for a while and I instantly started to remember the look on Jay's face, as we walked up the corridor on that first day, did my face look the same, was I the same ashen colour? I took a deep breath to try to calm down but within a few seconds, all of the feelings and emotions came flooding back and I was overwhelmed with the thoughts and fears of that scary word…cancer.

By the time I had gathered my thoughts, I felt ready to drive home but then the ultimate act of 'wearing a mask' followed, I had to walk into the house and act normal in front of my sons. I desperately wanted to tell them the truth, after all, they were old enough to understand but at the end of the day, I'm still their mum and my role is to protect them and I knew that telling them of the 'potential' only served to worry them so I decided to tell them when I knew more.

That day I reflected on my time with Jay, I remembered all the days we had to spend waiting for appointments, letters, results etc, the waiting is by far the cruellest part of being on a cancer pathway for both the patient and the loved ones, it's almost as bad as knowing bad news.

Over the following days, I switched on an hourly basis from being scared to positive, I wanted to cry but I found it hard, I wanted to be angry but didn't know who to be angry with. My partner it has to be said was and still is fantastic, sometimes he didn't need to say anything, he just held me and gave me a hug, which was exactly what I needed; however, I could see that he didn't really know how to be with me, he tried to be positive but there were times when I could see on his face that he was deep-down just as scared as me.

A few days later I went to visit Jay's grave; I just needed to talk to him. It was so peaceful at the Crematorium; the autumnal colours seemed to bring a warmth to the otherwise cold day, the leaves were blowing in the wind so all you could hear was a faint rustling sound as they blew around. For such a sad place it can often be an incredibly comforting place to be, for those moments you are there you can just block out the rest of the world and you focus solely on the person you are remembering, it's incredibly cathartic.

I know many people don't understand why people feel the need to visit a grave, they don't see how it helps as at the end of the day the loved one isn't there in person but to me, they are. I'm under no illusion, I know he's died but I really do take comfort in the fact that his spirit is there and I feel as close as I can be to him when I'm there. I don't feel that I have to go every week or even every month but having a place to go and talk and reflect is important to me and I take solace in that.

Chapter 40

The appointment to see the consultant took just under two weeks and I felt every single one of those days, it really did feel like every day was a week. Every day I would hypothesise the potential outcomes, both good and bad but if I'm honest, it was mostly the bad. I had age and health on my side, I was relatively young and I was relatively healthy so if it was cancer unless it was aggressive or a very late diagnosis, my chances were very good.

On the day of my appointment, I felt physically nauseous, my appointment wasn't until 15:30hrs so I had all day to wait, every second was a minute, every minute was an hour; it was a very, very long day. Driving to the hospital, I had no idea what the roads were like, all I could think about was how the day was going to end and what my diagnosis would look like, would it end in relief or would I be preparing for the fight of my life?

What made the day harder was that I was unable to take anyone with me for support. We were at the time in a second lockdown due to Covid-19 so the rules were that you had to go alone to all appointments.

I cannot imagine not being with Jay when he had all his appointments, I went with him to every single one; I never missed one throughout the whole of his journey. Having that support was part of the process and having someone there to hold his hand in both the good and bad news was a comfort beyond words but here I was, on my own and scared of what was about to happen.

The corridors of the hospital were familiar to me; they were the same corridors I used to walk to visit Jay when he was an in-patient throughout his many stays in hospital through sickness or surgeries. The emotions and the feelings were insurmountable but looking around I knew I had to find the courage to keep walking and to get through it as I knew there were many other people just like me in exactly the same situation, sometimes worse, so I knew I had to be strong.

I took my seat in the waiting room and after a few moments was called into the clinical room with a nurse; I was asked the usual medical questions and shown to the dressing area so I could change into the usual fetching hospital gown. This in itself was a trauma as I didn't actually know I was having any sort of treatment at this particular appointment. I had wrongly assumed that it was just a talk with the Oncology Consultant to discuss my case so to envisage having any sort of treatment today was a shock. I was shown through to the waiting area and I took a seat. Whilst I was scared and nervous, I also knew that if I had known what today held for me my anxiety about the appointment would have been a hundred times worse, so maybe not knowing was a good turn of events.

Before I left the changing cubicle, I just sat on the bench, *this was it, this was when my life was either going to be changed forever or it could all be okay and a false alarm.* I'm not particularly religious but it's at these times that I do sit quietly and just say a few words to God and at times to Jay too. I ask for support and for him to guide me, I have no idea really if it makes a difference but, in that moment, it offers a sense of calmness and serenity. I truly believe that in moments like that it is important to hold onto anything that gives you the strength to stand up and find a calmness in the storm.

Nervously, I made my way out of the changing cubicle and the nurse led me down to the treatment room. I was met by the consultant, a nurse and two students.

The procedure is not the nicest experience so as I twiddled my thumbs and tried to breathe the nurse could tell I was a bundle of nerves, she talked calmly to me and told me to try not to worry. I told her why I was worried and that I had come so far after losing Jay that being unwell myself was just not an option, I explained that I refused to tell my boys that another one of their parents had cancer.

Now, they say that you don't become a nurse, you are born one, and it's within their soul and their innate personality. A good nurse doesn't need to try to be nice, it comes out instinctively, their caring nature and thoughtful actions can often mean more to patients than the treatment itself at times.

Anyone reading this who has or is going through a cancer pathway either themselves or as a carer will have one thing in common and that is that we have all experienced the exceptional care of our NHS staff. The human kindness element of the journey is overwhelmingly important and if there are any health professionals reading this now, please be assured that your kindness and compassion is so appreciated and valued. Whilst your medical knowledge and expertise is what saves lives, it is that simple hug or those kind words which keep a person from falling and keeps them emotionally alive. You make a huge difference to people's lives and I am sure I speak on behalf of many others that we are so very grateful to each and every one of you.

After what felt like forever but was only really five-ten minutes, the consultant smiled and said the words I needed to hear, "Jo, its fine, it's not cancer." I simply cried, but due to Covid-19 restrictions, the nurses are not allowed any physical contact so she simply smiled, pulled the curtain around and let me have a moment so I could regain some composure.

Her kind words will stay with me forever, she just said, "You are going to be okay, it's good news Jo." I sat back down in the cubicle to get re-dressed and just kept whispering "thank you" to myself, I'm not sure who I was thanking but I was just incredibly grateful for being given the all-clear.

In all of this, one person was at the forefront of my mind and that was Jay. I kept taking myself back to his Endoscopy on day one, and imagining how he must have felt when I left him in the waiting room and how he felt when the consultant said he wanted to speak to us both when he had recovered. The face when he walked out of the doors towards me, the way he held my hand when we sat down in the office, the look on his face when the consultant told us the diagnosis, all of those emotions suddenly become very real and my admiration for Jay and his amazing tenacity was higher than ever before.

Having the experience of being the patient as well as the carer had been an eye-opening experience. If I'm honest if I were asked which experience was the worst, I'm not sure I could answer it as both experiences were emotional.

Chapter 41

The cancer journey is fraught with emotions, they range from elation to despair and despair to elation on a daily and weekly basis; it's hard to know what each day will bring. Everyone's journey is different, two people may have the exact same cancer but their experience is unique to them and to their loved ones. The caring for cancer journey cannot truly be conveyed in words, it is something that is felt, experienced and lived.

The journey is a roller-coaster, there are times when you feel exhilarated and overcome with happiness and there are times of intense fear and uncertainty, there are times when you feel strong and brave and you can confidently hold on knowing you have to get through it but equally there are times when you just want to scream at someone to stop and let you off and for it all to be over.

It's hard to give advice on what to do to survive the roller-coaster but if I can say one thing, it is simply to hold on and when someone offers to hold your hand for support, let them. Don't be afraid to be scared but equally don't be afraid to acknowledge the good times when you are able to smile, laugh and be positive. Those good times are amazing and no matter how small, they are incredibly important.

I know that I had to be strong but I also had to allow myself to be weak and to fall, I had to allow myself to be vulnerable and to accept the help that was offered. It was not easy at all but I did it.

When I fell down, I felt like I was falling onto a concrete floor, it felt hard and cold and I was constantly in pain but I now know that it really was part of the process and although it hurts you have to let it happen. When you are ready and only when you are ready, you can start to think about getting up and finding the strength you need to stand up again and to start to walk forward but…it takes time.

I know that I will always grieve for Jay; I know that I will always miss him but I also know that I have been given an opportunity to be happy again. I am so very grateful for my life and for all those people who stood by me and offered that hand of support when I needed it. I used to take that support for granted but I am indebted to that help now, I know how important it was in my recovery. Help comes in many different forms; it can be a supportive telephone call or a simple hug with not one word spoken.

Throughout writing this book, people have asked me why I wanted to share my experience. The answer is quite simple, I wanted people to know the raw truth, even if that meant laying my own heart on the line for everyone else to see.

Cancer is a truly devastating and cruel disease and whilst modern medicine has developed at an extraordinary rate, it is still responsible for thousands of deaths each year. Research is crucial if scientists are to find a cure but while they continue in their quest, we unfortunately, will continue to suffer the bereavement and loss of our loved ones.

My story is not one of negativity and upset, it is one of hope. I am just one of many who have suffered the loss of a loved one and I will sadly not be the last. From my experience, I hope that you can see that the journey can be long, it can be hard and it can be heart-breaking but it can also be full of laughter, hope and encouragement.

I still cry and I still feel sadness but I also feel like me again, I feel hope and I feel self-worth, those are emotions I never thought possible when I started this journey.

Jay walks with me still and even in my new journey he will be there watching over me and giving me strength, but for now, I proudly walk as a strong woman with my two sons, Gareth, my family and my friends at my side. I hold on to my past but I am now looking forward to a happy future.

Life is good again and I feel that I can be excited about the future. Now, for me, life is about watching my sons continue to flourish, maybe getting married themselves one day and who knows, future grandchildren! I look forward to my own wedding to Gareth which I know will be the start of a new chapter in my life and a whole new journey of possibilities.

If you are going through a similar journey or you know someone who is, it is so important to acknowledge that with all of the darkness there is also light. With every bad day, there are good days and when you lose sight of the goals, take a breath, find your inner strength and take it slow.

Embrace the love and support you have around you but never lose sight of the life, you still lead and will still have in the future.

The End

Ending Words

There are many great attributes that can be associated with Britain, some anecdotal and some humorous, however when it comes to bereavement there is one quote in particular which summarises how some 'British' people would approach grief and bereavement, "Keep Calm and Carry On". This very famous quote can be used in a multitude of ways but in the case of how the British tackle dealing with difficult situations I think this is a fairly common thought-process.

The needs of a bereaved person can be both simple and complex, depending on the circumstances. Grief is a normal reaction to a loss and in 'normal' grief a person will work through their bereavement at their own pace and in their own way with little need for external support other than their family and friends, however there are others for whom the grief will be more complex and will need additional support.

Identifying the needs of a bereaved person can be difficult at first as it requires the bereaved person to recognise that they do need help with moving towards more restorative thinking rather than loss-orientated thinking. The person may not believe that they need support and may challenge any involvement, regardless of how well-meant the suggestion is.

British society in general favours towards us all being overly tenacious and stoic with an ultra-resilience to adversity and whilst this is not the rule for many it is still a factor in many people.

Death is essentially unavoidable and therefore bereavement will always be prominent in society, it is something which should be given priority in respect of emotional wellbeing and ongoing mental health care as with good support people can and do work through their grief and are able to adapt and move on in their lives.

It is important to remember that bereavement is not an illness it is a reaction to grief and whilst it can manifest in very real physiological and psychological symptoms, they are all entirely normal and part of the tasks of mourning. British society in general needs to be highlighting that in the event of a death, it is okay to be sad and to experience the emotions associated with the loss of a loved one and that it is in fact more harmful to 'bottle up the feelings' and overlook the innate need to grieve.

I believe that there is almost a stigma attached to death in that it is a taboo subject which best be avoided in order to avoid any negative consequences, however if we all actually talked about death, we would increase our awareness and be able to identify those who are struggling after a bereavement.

Recognising the needs of bereaved people is reliant on people understanding the range of reactions which may be evident and knowing what support can be offered if they do want to help. Acquiring the knowledge of how to help and then signposting that person to the available services is key to helping bereaved people and this can happen in many ways such as leaflets or posters in prominent areas such as GP waiting rooms, supermarkets, hospitals etc. By recognising the need of the bereaved we can better support them and their futures.

The great British 'Keep Calm and Carry on' philosophy may be good witticism however in reality we need to be recognising that grieving is not straight-forward and even the most resilient of people can sometimes need support. Eliminating the stigma attached to asking for help and increasing awareness are key to ensuring that the needs of bereaved people are met.

My experience has been complex and full of an array of different feelings and emotions; however, it has also been full of insightfulness and hope; my experience has taught me that life is a journey and it is full of twists and turns but ultimately from something which is initially negative it can be transformed into positive enlightenment.

Grief is not easy, it cannot be rushed, nor can it be ignored, it is the pain of grief which ultimately gets us through those emotional times and is also the grief that makes us stronger.